WITHDRAWN

Who Paid
for
Modernism?

Who Paid
for
Modernism?

ART, MONEY, AND
THE FICTION OF
CONRAD, JOYCE, AND LAWRENCE

Joyce Piell Wexler

THE UNIVERSITY OF ARKANSAS PRESS
FAYETTEVILLE 1997

01 00 99 98 97   5 4 3 2 1

Designed by Ellen Beeler

☉ The paper used in this publication meets the minimum requirements of the
American National Standard for Permanence of Paper for Printed Library Materials
Z39.48-1984.

Library of Congress Cataloging-in-Publication Data

Wexler, Joyce Piell, 1947–
    Who paid for modernism : art, money, and the fiction of Conrad, Joyce, and
Lawrence / Joyce Piell Wexler.
        p.   cm.
    Includes bibliographical references (p.   ) and index.
    ISBN 1-55728-445-8 (cloth : alk. paper)
        1. English fiction—20th century—History and criticism. 2. Modernism
(Literature)—Great Britain. 3. Novelists, English—20th century—Economic
condition. 4. Fiction—Authorship—Economic aspects—Great Britain.
5. Capitalism and literature—Great Britain—History—19th century. 6. Conrad,
Joseph, 1857–1924—Authorship. 7. Joyce, James, 1882–1941—Authorship.
8. Lawrence, D.H. (David Herbert), 1885–1930—Authorship. 9. Authors and
publishers—Great Britain—History—20th century. 10. Authors and readers—
Great Britain—History—20th century. I. Title.
PR888.M63W43 1997
823'.912091—dc20   96-33005
                                                                              CIP

For Jerome again

Acknowledgments

This project began many years ago in the archives of Northwestern University. I want to thank Samuel Hynes for directing me to the papers of the literary agency founded by James Brand Pinker. I am grateful, also, to the firm of Chadwyck-Healey Limited for underwriting the initial sorting of boxes filled with the miscellaneous papers a literary agency collects in thirty years of doing business by mail. Russell Maylone and the Department of Special Collections at Northwestern University provided me with company, encouragement, and space for this work. Early versions of several chapters have appeared in *Studies in the Novel, Sewanee Review, Conradiana, The D. H. Lawrence Review,* and *Marketing Modernisms,* edited by Kevin J. H. Dettmar and Stephen Watt. J. A. Sutherland read a draft and encouraged my study, which is modeled on his *Victorian Novelists and Publishers.* William J. Veeder also offered important advice. My colleague David Chinitz read the nearly completed manuscript and made detailed and valuable suggestions. This is an opportunity, also, to thank those who have made everything possible—my parents, my husband, and my daughters.

Contents

Introduction: Art v. Money

> *Goethe shrugged and said with some pride, "Perhaps our books*
> *are immortal, in a certain sense. Perhaps." He paused and then*
> *added softly, with great emphasis, "But we aren't."*
> *"Quite the contrary," Hemingway protested bitterly. "Our*
> *books will probably soon stop being read. . . . But people will never*
> *stop prying into your life, down to the smallest details." (213–14)*
> —MILAN KUNDERA, *IMMORTALITY*

Kundera's imagined conversation between Goethe and Hemingway
illustrates our tenacious interest in the lives of famous writers. Authors
may be dead, literally and theoretically, yet we continue to believe
that the literature we value is grounded in the lives of the people who
wrote it. Although it now seems tautological to attribute canonical
work to the "genius" of the writer, we continue to seek the source
of the work in the author's life. Kundera makes his point ironically
by using a German Romantic writer to affirm the value of the work
in itself and an American modernist to assert the public's greater
interest in the writer's life. While Romantics assumed that their work
originated in their own experience, they also believed that art had
enduring social value. And modernists may have sought impersonality, but they also knew that their lives were part of their literary
reputation.[1] Roland Barthes makes this point more generally in
"From Work to Text": the author's "life is no longer the origin of
his fables, but a fable that runs concurrently with his work. There is
a reversal, and it is the work which affects the life, not the life which
affects the work: the work of Proust and Genet allows us to read their
lives as a text" (78–79).

Although Joseph Conrad, James Joyce, and D. H. Lawrence
strived to make their fiction impersonal, their personal lives have

become part of the myth of modernism. Conrad's years at sea, Joyce's bohemian exile, and Lawrence's autobiographical references make readers feel that these authors' narratives are authentic representations of real life. But the reverse is true. It is the characters who retroactively endow their authors with glamour. Modernists and their biographers have taught us to read their lives as we do their fiction, but another story remains untold: to become published authors in the first place, they had to reconcile competing models of authorship, and their fiction bears the scars of this struggle.

Despite their aesthetic of impersonality, modernist authors' professional strategy depended on self-promotion. Their dilemma was rooted in an ideological contradiction between art and money that pervaded their culture, as it continues to dominate our own. This contradiction posed the Romantic ideal of the writer as genius who expressed an inviolable inner vision without regard for its rhetorical effect or market value against a newer definition of the author as professional who earned a living by writing. Moreover, each ideal generated cautionary counterparts. The specter of the artist who wrote for himself was the amateur who wrote for no one else; the underside of the professional was the hack who wrote only for money. The modernist writer had to steer a course between both figures of contempt. The careers of Conrad, Joyce, and Lawrence illustrate the effects of these competing models. All three writers used the myth of the artist to further their professional careers; they had to conceal their professional aims to maintain their aesthetic reputations. While definitions of modernism and lists of modernists vary, these three writers illustrate a range of modernist responses to an ideology that held art and money to be antithetical.

By the early twentieth century, the artist's need to renounce a popular audience was a commonplace, and each of these writers found a model of professionalism opposed to popularity in Flaubert. To varying degrees, all three accepted his argument that impersonality was the proper narrative stance for the serious novelist and that control of point of view was the formal expression of this position. With his aesthetic views, they absorbed his conception of the novelist as professional. Most writers who earned their living as novelists thought of themselves as professional authors, but Flaubert tried to exclude those who wrote bestsellers and earned a great deal of money from his stricter definition of the term. His idea of the professional was an expert whose talent could only be judged by peers. To be concerned with payment was beneath his dignity, though as a professional he was entitled to receive a fee for services. Nevertheless, earning money remained an essential part of the model of the professional author. Notwithstanding their rhetoric of martyrdom, Conrad, Joyce, and Lawrence began their careers with the aspiration of becoming not only artists but also authors who earned their living by writing. Each found a commercial publisher with his first submission, and each had far more financial success than he liked to admit. Despite the economic success of their work in their lifetimes, however, their careers have been interpreted as evidence of society's neglect of greatness. Since biographies and collected letters are available for all three writers, it is possible to trace the development of their aesthetic ideas in relation to their publishing experiences.

The expansion of literacy in the nineteenth century made wealth a possibility for authors, but sales jeopardized critical acclaim. Popularity became a sign of aesthetic compromise, and lack of material success became the defining quality of the modernist artist. Renato Poggioli articulates the issues at stake in the modernist myth when he claims that the opportunity for "financial success to a point simply unthinkable in earlier times or societies" has caused "the frequent and usually sincere refusal, on the part of the real artist in our day, to give in to the lure of material success. Furthermore, even if he allows himself to be tempted, the artist can only put his trust in chance or luck because the public he wishes to reach is not reducible to a definite entity or to a series of classifiable groups—thanks to its great numbers, the complexity of its needs and the variations in its structure" (675). Poggioli sees money as a temptation to sell out rather than as a reward for creating something valuable to others. Refusing payment becomes a sign of aesthetic integrity, which is defined in opposition to qualities that the popular audience values. At the same time, he realizes that the public is too diverse to manipulate.

Poggioli points out that the avant-garde model of the alienated artist presupposes an oppositional relationship to bourgeois society:

"*Avant-garde* art, as a minority culture, must attack and deny the majority culture to which it is opposed" (670). Contrasting the alienated artist with the Romantic paradigm, Poggioli notes that although Wordsworth accepted the rhetorical challenge of developing an audience (stating that "every poet must create the taste by which he is to be enjoyed"), for "the modern genius" this was "an enormous undertaking, futile and also impossible" (677). Whereas Romantic artists discovered Promethean power in alienation, the modern avant-garde artist was conceived as a sacrificial lamb: "In this way the poet or artist, having fallen from the position of the elect to that of the rejected . . . assumes, in turn, the new roles of saint and martyr"(673). Even in a secular age, these religious terms enforce the antithesis between art and money. Money became a temptation, and popularity became a sign of moral weakness. Despite Poggioli's idealization of the Romantic artist, among Wordsworth's reasons for developing an audience was the desire to sell his poems. John Feather notes the practical interests of Romantic writers: "The concern with copyright law . . . was one measure of the ever-increasing sums of money which could be generated by successful books, both for the author and for the publisher" (174). Romantic aesthetic statements are silent on the subject of payment, but Wordsworth and Southey lobbied to increase copyright benefits for authors (Feather 171).

The myth of the suffering artist is much older than modernism, but the modernists' situation was unique because any financial success they might have eventually achieved would have undermined their status as serious artists. Convinced that the pluralism of mass culture has "only a negative function" (684), Poggioli supports Sartre's judgment of the "historical uniqueness of this negative relationship": "'the drastic blurring of levels in the public since 1848 has caused the author initially to write against all readers'" (685). The diversity of the audience meant that bestsellers had to address readers at the lowest level. Although Poggioli defines the "real artist" as the creator of minority art, in opposition to the writer who produces bestsellers, the morality of the author's decision is moot because, as Poggioli warns, the audience is so complex that no writer can know it well enough to please it. Books succeed only by "chance or luck." What he calls chance or luck amounts to a fortuitous fit between writer and reader. Although serious and popular authors sometimes tried to appeal to the other group's audience, the attempt to imitate the other's strategy usually failed. Apparently, the fit between author and audience was beyond their control.

Poggioli's assessment summarizes the common assumptions that shaped modernist writers' careers: since the mass audience cannot appreciate quality, writers who aspire to aesthetic quality must renounce high sales. Furthermore, the audience is unknowable and cannot be sought directly. The corollaries are that whatever the mass audience likes must be junk, the writer who has a wide audience must have sold out, and authors who seek readers directly must be hacks. The ideology that pitted art against money meant that writers had to choose between them.

But the artist's economic condition was also subject to the competing model of the professional. In *Discovering Modernism,* Louis Menand argues that the professionalization of art in the late nineteenth century transformed literary careers. He connects aestheticism to the trend toward specialization in other kinds of work: just as managers took over from the industrial entrepreneur, professional authors displaced the literary genius. If authorship is like other professions, it has an economic motive and can be analyzed by asking, "Who paid for modernism?"

If seeking money was a temptation, failing to earn it was worse. It was hard to distinguish a starving artist from an unpublished amateur. Modernists could escape this dilemma by disclaiming interest in money and addressing a minority audience who could not be expected to provide a large income. Making their art difficult, they could not be mistaken for hacks. Since they ostentatiously refused to court a popular audience, they could accept any profits their work brought them. This shift from writing for a public to addressing a coterie was possible because an avant-garde audience eager to distinguish itself from the popular audience emerged.

Conrad was surprised to discover that his desire for the income of popular authors conflicted with his artistic aims. When he decided to become a writer, he assumed that art and sales were compatible goals; with experience, he recognized the need to choose between them, or to appear to choose between them. Conrad himself felt his purpose was always both aesthetic and rhetorical, but critics assumed that his less popular books were written with more integrity than his bestsellers. The high sales of *Chance* in 1913 proved an embarrassment to his early admirers; since it was popular, critics reasoned, he must have compromised his art.

For Joyce and Lawrence, legal issues of censorship due to libel and obscenity delayed commercial publication. Censorship justified their protests that they were persecuted, but it also advertised illicit fiction and ultimately increased sales. Modernists found that opposition to bourgeois morality brought the supreme bourgeois reward: money. Censorship made it possible for Joyce to create a myth of himself as a martyr to his art, a myth that continues to govern our image of him. Lawrence also provoked censorship, but he defended the explicit sexuality in his fiction as part of his moral purpose rather than as artistic necessity.[2] Both found patrons who helped them circumvent legal obstacles. Although these private publishers offered financial support, their decisions were not based on superior literary insight but on a political commitment to protest censorship and a desire to be part of an avant-garde coterie.

The dichotomy between art and money also moralized common rhetorical intentions: self-expression was idealized as integrity, and communication was demonized as selling out. The classical discipline of rhetoric as the art of persuasion had an obvious social purpose, and the rhetorical defense of art in terms of its moral effect on the audience had a distinguished history. But when Flaubert refused to allow the audience's response to measure the value of his work, the reader's response lost its importance. The aestheticism of the 1890s and the "art for art's sake" slogan exacerbated the artist's contempt for popular opinion and bourgeois morality. By the end of the nineteenth century, "rhetoric" was a term of abuse. Aspects of authorship that had been complementary for Victorian authors seemed mutually exclusive. Modernist writers felt that the rhetorical concerns associated with being a professional author were incompatible with the aesthetic aims of being a serious artist, yet they could not renounce either model. As artists, modernists were committed to resisting social demands, but as authors they also had to find publishers and readers. Writing with the reader's response in mind acquired the pejorative connotations of manipulation and exploitation.

In *Writing Degree Zero* Barthes argues that Flaubert's claims to the rights of craftsmanship transformed the serious writer's relation to the audience. Flaubert marked the origin of the antithesis between popularity and aesthetic integrity. He insisted that the value of writing should be measured not by its usefulness to the reader but by the effort it cost the writer. As a craftsman, he wanted "work-value" to replace "usage-value" (62–63). To prevent his own art from becoming one more commodity, Flaubert tried to impose intricate controls on readers through the text to compensate for his inability to control what happened to his books after publication. Implicit in this was Flaubert's unwillingness to have his writing evaluated by ordinary readers. Only his peers could pass judgment.

Flaubert asserted that authors were independent of the reading audience, but he based his claim on professional expertise rather than genius. An audience of other writers would ensure higher standards than ordinary readers could be expected to maintain. Flaubert denied that art could be judged by sales and insisted instead that the artist should be judged as a professional. He based his rhetorical ideal on a growing professional class distinct from both owners and workers; the expertise and credentials of professionals protected them from raw market conditions (Menand 114). Although money was taboo in Flaubert's defense of the artist, professionals expected to be paid for specialized skills. Like members of other professions, writers pretended that payment was a matter beneath their attention. As their fiction became more profitable, serious writers asserted their contempt for money more vehemently.

Pierre Bourdieu also traces the modernist conception of the author to Flaubert. Attributing the invention of pure aesthetics to Flaubert, Bourdieu regards the model of the alienated artist as a strategy for criticizing society. Flaubert staked out the "art for art's sake" position in contrast to "social art," which was committed to political change, and "bourgeois art," which served domestic morality. Bourdieu proposes that literature should be considered a field of multiple forces that actors and institutions affect. Without resorting to biography, he considers authors as actors in a "space of *objective* relations between positions" (544). Bourdieu does not seek the genesis of literature in the biography of the writer's unique self, but instead relates publication to an author's career; that is, to a series of positions in the literary field.[3] In this field, art for art's sake was itself a social position: "Although it never excluded a good deal of posturing (namely, Baudelaire), this attitude presupposed very particular dispositions, associated with positions and trajectories that favored distance with respect to the social world" (561).

Bourdieu minimizes the impact of the writer's unique, personal experiences on rhetorical decisions. Since individual psychology is itself a product of culture, he rejects "the ideology of the 'man of genius' . . . which seeks the explanatory principle of a work in the author taken in isolation (the uniqueness of a work being considered a characteristic of the 'creator'). In fact, this explanatory principle resides in the relationship between the 'space' of works in which each particular work is taken and the 'space' of authors in which each cultural enterprise is constituted" (539–40). This space provides a choice of options in the differential field literary culture provides in any period. To become an author, a writer must convince an editor that a text will have meaning for enough readers to make publication profitable. To achieve this end, most manuscripts require and receive detailed criticism from editors. In the modernist period, both authors and publishers knew that the prestige of critical esteem could be converted to sales.

If inferior writers were popular, unpopularity would be a badge of superior talent. Bourdieu analyzes the rationale Flaubert and his circle used: "[T]he tenants of pure art were destined to deferred gratification. Some, like Leconte de Lisle, went so far as to see in immediate success 'the mark of intellectual inferiority'" (553). Since popularity implied pandering, the successful bourgeois novelist was an even greater enemy than the bourgeois: "This concern to keep distant from all social sites implied the refusal to be guided by the public's expectations" (552). Low sales, therefore, became a sign of artistic integrity. Of course, writers with no talent were also able to invoke this argument as a defense against criticism.

Flaubert invented the modern artist as the "full-time professional, dedicated to his work, indifferent to the exigencies of politics as to the injunctions of morality" (Bourdieu 551). This need to define the professional artist in opposition to the bourgeois artist split art from money: "The more the artist asserted himself as an artist by asserting his autonomy, the more he turned 'the bourgeois' into the 'bourgeois,' the philistine. . . . . It was in effect an upside-down economy where the artist could win in the symbolical arena only by losing in the economic one (at least in the short term) and vice versa" (Bourdieu 553). Although Bourdieu contrasts the bourgeois novelist with Flaubert's "professional" writer, bourgeois novelists thought of themselves as professionals because they earned money writing. Flaubert's dichotomy between economic success and critical esteem hounded modernist novelists, but like Flaubert, they responded by accumulating what Bourdieu calls "cultural capital" and by developing their "authority as tastemakers" (547).

Modernists' use of the term "rhetoric" as a pejorative epithet for a particular kind of writing implies that rhetorical effect can be transcended, that true artists can disregard readers and create "art for art's sake," but this position enshrines a tautology. Publication is always a social event. Bourdieu cautions that "we ought to guard against reducing this fundamentally ambiguous process to its alienating effects as did Raymond Williams who in analyzing the English romantics simply forgot that this process had liberating effects as well" (547). Like Williams, most critics interested in connections between literature and money, whether on the left or the right, believe that capitalism is repressive, but in the modernist period radical art thrived. Commercial publishers bought manuscripts that attacked their values and addressed minority audiences.

Each author's conception of his audience is apparent in his choice of narrative point of view. Conrad, Joyce, and Lawrence all explicitly acknowledged their debt to Flaubert in forming their aesthetic aims. His conception of the art novel made technical control of point of view the defining characteristic of serious modernist fiction: "It is one of my principles that a writer should not be his own theme. An artist must be in his work like God in creation, invisible and all-powerful; he should be everywhere felt, but nowhere seen. Furthermore, Art must rise above personal emotions and nervous susceptibilities. It is time to endow it with pitiless method, with the exactness of the physical sciences" (Flaubert 195). Flaubert's method of free indirect discourse focalizes the narrative from a character's perspective, using the character's style of thinking and speaking while avoiding both a first-person and an omniscient point of view. As a result of Flaubert's theory and practice, an impersonal point of view became a test of formal sophistication, yet eventually most modernist novelists deviated from a strict Flaubertian stance to compensate for the distance they felt between themselves and their readers. Conrad created Marlow, Joyce multiplied centers of consciousness, and Lawrence returned to an omniscient perspective to represent the unconscious.

Fredric Jameson connects the impersonal narrative point of view in modernist fiction to the writer's inability to identify the reader. He also recognizes Flaubert as the "privileged locus" of the disappearance of the text's "readership, which will become the *public introuvable* of modernism" (220–21). Jameson notes the "primacy of the Jamesian narrative category of point of view" in the modernist aesthetic, which derived from Flaubert (219–20). Henry James made narrative point of view the "most fundamental of narrative categories" and developed "a whole aesthetic" around it because he had to construct the reader within the text: "The subject having been by the logic of social development stripped from its textual object, the latter must now be constructed in such a way as to bear the place of the former within itself: the narrative becomes a tree-crashing sound that will remain *heard* even when the forest is empty, since its subject-pole, its organization by reception, is built into it" (221).

Jameson attributes the modernist "fragmentation of the psyche" (229) to reified vision and reified language under capitalism, but he realizes that the relationship is not simple mirroring: "That modernism is itself an ideological expression of capitalism, and in particular, of the latter's reification of daily life, may be granted a local validity. . . . Yet modernism can at one and the same time be read as a Utopian compensation for everything reification brings with it" (236). While Jameson argues that modernism both expresses the ideology of capitalism and offers compensations for it, it is also important to recognize that the economic conditions of capitalism sustained the production of modernist art, and not merely as oppression generates resistance. Capitalism promoted modernism by producing a diversity of books that allowed segments of the reading public to choose freely. The market's refusal to impose an elite's preferences did not restrict the liberty of readers, but it limited the income of elite authors.

As intermediaries between writers and readers, publishers contributed to writers' conceptions of readers. Modernists' publishing experiences, including acceptance or rejection of manuscripts, editing, reviews, and sales, gradually altered their rhetorical aims. The following chapters examine the effect of these experiences on the fiction of Conrad, Joyce, and Lawrence, not as publishing history but as a study of the ways ideology and models of authorship interact with social institutions to shape literary texts. This approach attempts to account for these writers' literary production in terms of their conceptions of authorship rather than their personal lives. I depend on letters to contrast standard biographical accounts with these authors' explicit intentions. The letters articulate each author's conception of his audience in relation to his work and its publishing prospects. This approach also assumes that what makes readers respond to texts has more to do with what authors absorb from their culture than what is unique in their private lives. Each of these writers had to negotiate the dichotomy of art and money to develop his career.

An archive of papers that belonged to the firm of J. B. Pinker, one of the first literary agents in England, demonstrates the impact of the ideological antithesis between art and money. This collection of business documents from 1895 to 1934 reveals a network of transactions associated with publication. Letters from editors, newspaper and magazine syndicators, lawyers, tax collectors, insurance salesmen, translators, and reviewers supplement correspondence from once popular authors, aspiring writers who never sold a story, and canonical figures like Conrad, Joyce, and Lawrence, who were all Pinker's clients. As disparate as these items are, collectively they indicate that antithetical models of authorship were so pervasive that they appear where least expected. Defying any simplistic assumptions of self-interest, commercial publishers were eager to attract serious writers who addressed small audiences; serious writers were interested in sales; bestselling writers were interested in form and art. The opposition between "art" written for oneself and "hack work" written for an audience concealed the rhetorical aims and financial ambitions of modernists.

The actual lives of published writers had less effect on the image of the author than the widespread social need for a figure to express the period's ideal of individualism. The image of the author as artist promised freedom from the constraints that bound other citizens; creative work escaped the regimen, hierarchy, and reward structure of most jobs. An extreme example of the belief that it was necessary to live like an artist to be one appears in the Pinker papers. A desperate writer, unable to sell his work, begged Pinker to lend him money to buy a midwife's kit to deliver his own child. Seeking an ordinary job was out of the question because his identity as a writer depended on earning a living by his pen.

The demand for new texts is endless because publishers need new products to sell. The expressive ideology of art is so pervasive, however, that it intrudes on sociological analyses of publishing. Since authors receive payment, Robert Escarpit compares publication to prostitution: "To publish a work drawn from oneself for commercial reasons is a bit like prostituting oneself" ("Act of Publication" 396). The image of the artist as a genius who presents an inviolable vision also endures in the following account of the publishing process:

> The transformation of a writer with a manuscript into a novelist with a book and an audience thus involves producers, distributors, and promoters constitutive of a cultural apparatus beyond the writer's control yet essential to his or her purposes. Between writer and reader stand socially structured, "aesthetically irrelevant forces." In Arnold Hauser's terms, "a whole series of mediators and instruments of mediation" stands between creator and recipient; these "remove and alienate" artist and recipient from each other even while linking them. Mediating institutions make art less awesome and more accessible, but the demystification built into modern mediation involves a "deformation of the [artist's] creative vision." (Rogers 155)

This analysis of the means of distribution still idealizes the process of production. The sociological method falters when Hauser interprets the inevitable distance between writer and reader as alienation and characterizes any attempt to bridge it as a deformation. His position presupposes that aesthetic value transcends "socially structured" forces. It elevates the creation of art to an aesthetic realm entirely separate from a social reality. This opposition partakes of the ideology modernist writers inherited from the anti-bourgeois impersonalism of Flaubert. But no artist is so alienated that he or she exists outside a social reality; no aesthetic is possible outside a social definition. In Frederic Jameson's words, "the aesthetic act is itself ideological" (79). Since publishers also considered themselves professionals, negotiating contracts was difficult. Literary agents appeared in the 1890s because they were willing to discuss payment without shame—some would say shamelessly. Despite complaints from unpublished writers, the market produced more books than the public could buy. Legends of the neglect of now canonical modernist fiction were exaggerations, but they survived because the success of popular books made highbrow fiction seem marginal. Sales and quality were no longer linked because the reading public had expanded, and popularity depended on the largest, not the most discriminating, segment of the audience. Nevertheless, the minority public constituted a market, and commercial publishers immediately recognized the value of modernist fiction, although they knew it was unlikely to appeal to a wide audience. Routinely blamed for restricting access to art, publishers were more often responsible for bringing innovative fiction to the public. Publishing records demonstrate that modernist novelists were not indifferent to readers, and publishers were not philistines.

The image of the author as artist rather than professional not only formed these authors but also dictated the plot of their biographies. These authors cast themselves in the role of the artist as martyr, and their biographers have accepted this model. Biographical narratives emphasize the personal events that correspond to the fiction, and the author's life becomes part of the rhetorical effect of the text. But the plot itself conforms to the ideology modernists inherited; the biographies are not accounts of how these writers became famous authors. Operating in the same set of ideological contradictions as authors, biographers often argue that their subjects were indifferent to readers and profits to prove that they were devoted to art. Biographies tend to celebrate the defiance of the artist and minimize the labor of the professional. In the conflict between writing for oneself and writing for an audience, professionalism, profit, and rhetoric are aligned against art, martyrdom, and self-expression.

The major biographies of Conrad, Joyce, and Lawrence adhere

to the story of the suffering artist.[4] Since their purpose is to construct artistic reputations, biographers focus on their subjects' private feelings rather than their rhetorical intentions. The relationship between writers' lives and their work is the legitimate province of biography, yet psychological analysis of their lives and writing tends to exaggerate the importance of subjective sources and to minimize rhetorical objectives. Most biographers regard rhetorical decisions as aesthetic compromises because they are conscious and directed at the audience. Seeking the source of exceptional art in exceptional experiences, biographers tend to substitute the Freudian unconscious for Romantic inspiration as the sacred source of art beyond conscious control.

When read in the context of contemporary publishing practices, the evidence these biographies provide also shows that each novelist tried to attract a wide audience early in his career. In addition, collected editions of each author's letters published after the landmark biographies appeared complicate the model of modernist impersonality. In contrast to the portraits the biographies construct, the letters are like snapshots that catch authors in various moods. The novelists' letters express contradictory aims: sometimes they said they were writing for art, sometimes for money, sometimes for both.[5] While the biographies construct a plot that links private and unconscious sources to each writer's fiction, it is also possible to trace rhetorical intentions to cultural institutions. In their letters, these authors describe the rhetorical effect they hoped to produce, and in fact, their formal decisions determined the audience they reached. Publishing experiences shaped their conceptions of their audience, and their image of the reader influenced their rhetorical intentions. In contrast to their biographers, each writer believed formal control improved his work aesthetically and rhetorically.

When Joyce and Lawrence began to write, their expectations were similar to Conrad's, but their major works appeared during and after World War I, the great divide of the modernist period. Although the war stimulated the book trade, its effects on modernism were mixed. Operating in wartime conditions, publishers faced paper shortages, but the demand for books was so great at the front and at home that sales soared. Marie Belloc Lowndes, a bestselling author before the war, wrote J. B. Pinker, who was also her literary agent: "There is a great demand just now for 1/- books, I hear it on all sides" (Pinker Papers, 28 January 1915). And R. T. Jupp, a director at the London Film Company, reported, "The public taste is now all for heavier things" (Pinker Papers, 3 February 1915). The war prepared the public to accept the modernist critique of society that had begun earlier. As public taste veered toward serious subjects and poetry, prewar styles and subjects seemed as false and foolish to the popular audience as they had appeared to the avant-garde.

To demonstrate how the ideological pressures of the period shaped writers' conceptions of authorship, my discussion of the careers of Conrad, Joyce, and Lawrence emphasizes a different issue for each. Although Conrad adopted a philosophical position close to solipsism, he realized it threatened the social value of literature. His ambition to be both a professional writer and an artist depended on literature having a social function. Joyce's career illustrates the conflict between the artist's quest for unfettered freedom and the professional author's need to serve some social function. Lawrence's career struggles with the difficulty of reconciling the unconscious sources of art with a social purpose.

CHAPTER ONE

The Economics of the Starving Artist

"Art for art's sake" may have been modernists' legacy from the nineties, but it was not their own rhetorical position. Whereas aestheticism represses the relationship between author and reader, modernist form demands a confrontation with the audience. Although modernists were intensely aware of the effect of their writing on readers, they used "rhetoric" as an epithet for the kind of writing they opposed. Pound spoke for many modernists when he defined rhetoric as "loose expression" and "the loose use of individual words" (21). Similarly, Eliot endorsed contemporary poets' efforts to "escape the rhetorical, the abstract, the moralizing" ("Reflections" 118). Once rhetoric became a general term of opprobrium for inaccurate and unauthentic usage, however, rhetorical intention and rhetorical effect also became reprehensible concerns insofar as they implied an effort to attract readers. Modernists were contemptuous of writers—and anyone else—who courted a wide audience for profit. The dichotomy between literature as authentic oppositional language and rhetoric as false biased usage opened in this period, and we are only now beginning to find ways to bridge it.

The popular audience did not destroy the audience for serious fiction, but it did marginalize it. In 1891 Oscar Wilde perceived that the proliferation of books threatened art and urged critics to rescue it: "It is Criticism, again, that, by concentration, makes culture possible. It takes the cumbersome mass of creative work, and distils it into a finer essence. Who that desires to retain any sense of form could struggle through the monstrous multitudinous books that the world has produced, books in which thought stammers or ignorance brawls? The thread that is to guide us across the wearisome labyrinth is in the hands of Criticism" (216). Too much competition, not restriction of the market, endangered art.

By the 1930s, the situation Wilde described was so much worse that F. R. Leavis called upon "independent and intelligent critics" (38) to guide readers "amid the smother of new books" (32). Leavis defended the need to rely on a minority to make literary judgments: "Upon this minority depends our power of profiting by the finest human experience of the past; they keep alive the subtlest and most perishable parts of tradition. Upon them depend the implicit standards that order the finer living of an age . . ." (15). Leavis distrusted popular opinion as much as Flaubert did, but Leavis placed his trust in expert readers rather than expert writers.

Although critically esteemed fiction lost its former prominence in the crush of popular books, it continued to be published because it was profitable. As the literary market grew, the publishing industry eagerly penetrated all segments. The highbrow share was not the largest, but publishers were content with the minority novel's return on their investment. Minority authors, however, were not. While highbrow writers reiterated their disdain for money, the spectacle of inferior writers earning more than they did tormented them. Nevertheless, they refused to make their books more accessible merely to increase sales because such a decision would be, as both Joyce and Lawrence said, prostitution.[1] As a result of the stratification of the audience, sales were no longer accepted as an index of literary quality, but the tendency to equate money and value survived. To resist this equation, highbrow authors displaced their desire for sales onto the hack. Ambivalent about wanting a large audience, modernist writers insisted they wrote for themselves, yet they also needed some kind of validation to prove they were not merely aspiring amateurs.

Although modernists had to forfeit popularity to maintain aesthetic quality, the minority audience offered a kind of prestige unavailable to Victorian novelists. Instead of sales, the minority writer won access to elite circles of fame, luxury, and power. Social access did not pay the rent, but it did confirm the importance of modernist writing at a time when sales could not. Pierre Bourdieu's concept of "cultural capital" acknowledges the value of this kind of recognition. Assessing the social position of the avant-garde artist, Malcolm Bradbury similarly observes, "The literary life in our society is alluring, both to writers and readers, both as fact and fantasy, for several reasons: for the exemplary freedom it seems to offer, the possibilities for rapid social advancement it allows, and the changes of prestige, culturally or financially, that it can bring" (145). Conrad, Joyce, and Lawrence found these benefits in literature.

Writers who admitted that they wanted a large audience and the income it generated endangered their artistic reputations. Despite this tacit rule of literary culture, modernist writers were not indifferent to their readers when they began to write. Like the previous generation of novelists who were both successful and respected, writers such as Henry James, Thomas Hardy, and Arnold Bennett, modernists wanted to expand the genre's form and subject matter in original ways. Transgressing accepted literary forms and moral standards was the usual way for serious novelists to attract readers. Exposing hypocrisy and undercutting established forms had been a defining characteristic of the novel as a genre since the days of Richardson, Fielding, and Smollett (Rogers 62). One of the features that had always distinguished literature from popular fiction was that it "may seriously challenge one's attitudes and values" (Mann 355). Modernists expected to continue in this tradition, until they found that art and popularity were antithetical aims. Only after failing to attract as wide an audience as they felt they deserved did modernists make their texts difficult.

Authors

The modernists' dilemma was that popularity was both a goal and a trap. They had lost their predecessors' confidence that the common reader would understand them, yet they hoped to reach a wide audience. Despite the cold comfort of past cases of neglected genius acclaimed posthumously, the more recent example of Victorian poets and novelists who had achieved enormous popularity as well as critical esteem challenged modernist writers to prove themselves in both arenas. In *Victorian Novelists and Publishers,* J. A. Sutherland describes Thackeray, Dickens, Eliot, and Hardy earning artistic liberty by demonstrating their ability to achieve both critical and commercial success. Expressing the Victorian consensus, George Henry Lewes explicitly linked literary merit and commercial success: "Success, temporary or enduring, is the measure of the relation, temporary or enduring, which exists between a work and the public mind" (10). Writing in 1865, Lewes recognized the volatility of public taste: "Public knowledge and public taste fluctuate; and there come times when works which were once capable of instructing and delighting thousands lose their power, and works, before neglected, emerge into renown. A small minority to whom these works appealed has gradually become a large minority, and in the evolution of opinion will perhaps become the majority" (12). His description of the curve of the steady seller in the Victorian period also fits the actual reception of modernist fiction. As Lewes's principle predicts, modernist fiction gradually found a minority and then a majority audience. Most of the names on Pinker's list of the highest paid serial writers in 1914 are obscure today: Alice Williamson, H. G. Wells, E. Phillips Oppenheim, Perceval Gibbon, A. M. S. Hutchinson, Clayton Calthrop, and Marie Belloc Lowndes (Pinker Papers, *Nash's Magazine*, 5 January 1914). By 1929, however, an editor at Constable sent Pinker a list of the clients the firm wanted to publish that included James Joyce, Robert Graves, Constance Garnett, and Rebecca West (Pinker Papers, 2 April 1929).

Modernists could not accept Lewes's comfortable correlation between literary and commercial success. As professional authors, they had to earn a living, and as serious artists, they believed their work was too important to be limited to a coterie. At times, modernist writers explicitly sought as many readers as possible. Conrad told Edward Garnett, his first editor, "I *won't* live in an attic!" (Garnett 9). Joyce proclaimed that his intention in *Dubliners* was to give the Irish people "one good look at themselves in my nicely polished looking-glass" (*Selected Letters* 90). In letters to his agent in 1920

Joyce was still "describing his efforts to reach a wider audience," this time for *Ulysses* (E.L.A. 22).[2] Lawrence frankly sought a wide audience. His credo demanded one, and he believed he would eventually succeed: "And I shall get my reception, if not now, then before long" (Boulton 2:183–84). However alienated they were from conventional society, modernist writers nevertheless sought acclaim from readers. They expected literary fame to confer social status, and it did. Despite their complaints that they were paid less than inferior authors, Conrad, Joyce, and Lawrence actually earned more as writers than they would have been able to earn in any other career open to them at the time.[3]

As the potential audience for fiction grew, the possibility of achieving huge sales tempted writers to abandon their aesthetic principles and appeal to the broadest taste.[4] Ideological pressure made them exaggerate this temptation; selling out was harder than they realized. Books like *New Grub Street* and the manifestoes of little magazines made the author's internal conflict seem a practical choice, but even popular fiction had to obey what Lewes called the "Principle of Sincerity" to be successful (20). That is, there had to be a rhetorical match between author and reader: "This is not luck, but a certain fitness between the author's mind and the public needs" (9).

Conforming to another public's conventions was hard at both ends of the scale. Attempting to imitate popular formulas, both Conrad and Wyndham Lewis assured their agent, J. B. Pinker, they were following the recipe for potboilers, but they failed as miserably as Pinker's commercial clients, popular writers like Barry Pain and Alice Williamson, who told Pinker they wanted to incorporate avant-garde forms.[5] When an editor at Methuen criticized *Faloo* for its "brutal cynicism," Pain wrote Pinker, "I cannot be continually slipping in between my characters and the reader. The position of the author is not on the stage of his story—not even if he puts on a surplice for the purpose" (Pinker Papers, 16 July 1909). An agent of the Amalgamated Press complained to Pinker, "What *is* happening to Mrs. Williamson? I want stories told in a straight-forward way. This 'present-tense' and 'tricky' stuff will do neither Mrs. Williamson, nor the magazines any good" (Pinker Papers, 4 May 1928).

Modernist writers, however, felt torn between their artistic integrity and their professional need for public validation. Inheriting the Romantic definition of vocation as an inspired calling and the Victorian conception of vocation as remunerative work, modernist writers felt they had to prove the quality of their fiction by earning money writing, yet they could not sully the purity of their vision by deliberately altering it to win readers. Modernists' characteristic solution to the need to reconcile art and professionalism was to make their work difficult. Joyce is the prime example here: by the time he wrote *Finnegans Wake* he had abandoned the Irish people for "that ideal reader suffering from an ideal insomnia" (Ellmann 703). Once they could not reach a wide public, many modernist writers sought approval in self-selected coteries (Bradbury 207–8). An aesthetic of difficulty allowed writers to justify their need to publish while denying they wrote for readers.

In "The Culture of Modernism" Irving Howe indicates the hegemony of this characteristic: "The kind of literature called modern is almost always difficult; that is a sign of its modernity. To the established guardians of culture, the modern writer seems willfully inaccessible" (3). Howe traces the genealogy of the avant-garde artist's rhetorical stance to Hegel: "If there is then 'a conflict between a genius and his public,' declares Hegel . . . 'it must be the public that is to blame . . . the only obligation the artist can have is to follow truth and his genius'" (8). Howe invokes Hegel to justify any conflict between the writer and the audience as a byproduct of the writer's fidelity to art, but modernists made conflict with the reader central to their intentions.

Howe's aesthetic rationale is compatible with the mimetic defense that difficulty reflected the *Zeitgeist*. In T. S. Eliot's formulation in *"Ulysses,* Order, and Myth," *Ulysses,* Yeats, and presumably *The Waste Land,* had to use myth, however difficult it might be for readers, as a "way of controlling, of ordering, of giving a shape and a significance to the immense panorama of futility and anarchy which is contemporary history" (177). More emphatically, in "The Metaphysical Poets," he writes: "We can only say that it appears likely that poets in our civilization, as it exists at present, must be *difficult*" (65). Notwithstanding this orthodox defense, obscurity had other advantages.

The difficulty of modernist fiction allowed writers to express disdain for a wide audience. Many critics have recognized that this aesthetic pose of contempt conceals anxiety, but few have seen the professional interests beneath it. Julian Symons, for example, illustrates a common form of the myth that modernists accepted unpopularity as an element of artistic integrity:

> The fact that their writing was unlikely to be popular was accepted by the men of 1914. They were the first writers not just to exemplify the split in literary culture between "Highbrow" and "Lowbrow" that had begun in 1850 with the publication of the pre-Raphaelite *The Germ*, the first "little" magazine, but also consciously to accept that division. They may have wished for a wide readership, but knew they were not likely to get it. They were not writing for money. (70–71)

Overlooking the rhetorical effect of difficulty, Symons and other critics have praised modernist writers as incarnations of Stephen Dedalus.

Harry Levin provides a more extreme example of this tendency to hagiography in "What Was Modernism?":

> But popularity was excluded, by definition, from the aims of the writers I have been discussing; their names did not figure upon the best-seller lists of their day; many others did, which are now forgotten. The aura of obscurity or unintelligibility which may still occasionally tinge these intellectuals, in some degree, emanates from their refusal to advertise themselves or to talk down to their audience in the hope of enlarging it. (292)

And since modernists did not have to make "commitments" to the common welfare, "they could strive for artistic perfection in single-minded detachment" (293). Levin's view of the artist reflects the enduring assumption that a writer's concern with the effect of a work on the reader compromises its aesthetic value. The tendency of Symons and Levin to reason from the obscurity of late work backward to the writer's early intentions has concealed the fact that modernist writers did not always seek "singleminded detachment," even if such a position were possible.

Although the difficulty of modernism was an effective way to express disdain for popularity, difficulty has its own rhetorical effect. Despite its initial rebuff, formal complexity does not necessarily indicate that the author disregards the reader. It stipulates an audience prepared to work at interpretation as the author labored at composition. As a corollary of Flaubert's demand to be evaluated as a craftsman—according to the effort expended—the reader's work was also a mark of integrity. The value of a text was to be measured by the effort needed to construe it as well as to create it. Thus, modernists' response to the ideological dichotomy between art and money contributed to their obscurity, and obscurity attracted avant-garde readers.

This audience appeared because the forces that made some writers want to distinguish themselves from popular authors also made some readers eager to distinguish themselves from the popular audience. Despite these authors' periodic claims that they wrote for themselves, the culture that formed them produced their audience, an influential minority that also wanted to flout conventions. However authentic, deep, and intense their aesthetic response may have been, it was available only to an audience already in possession of certain assets, including sophisticated taste, erudition, and leisure. Difficulty undermines the economic position of the minority writer but preserves the cultural capital Bourdieu promises.

Publishers

No less than modernist writers, publishers had both mercenary and aesthetic interests. We are so willing to bemoan the sacrifice of art and morality to money—in Pound's words, to curse the "stranglehold that s.o.b. [i.e., commercial publishers] had on ALL publication" (Ford 215)—that we rarely examine how the publishing business operates. Throughout the modernist period, the financial interest of a publisher did not depend on bestsellers. It was more profitable for a firm to issue many books aimed at various segments of the market than to invest heavily in a few titles.

Because profits vary with costs, publishers had an incentive for supporting minority fiction. Although it addressed only the most literate segment of the market, original work by unpublished writers or writers whose work sold slowly could be bought more cheaply than a manuscript by an established writer. A cheap manuscript by a serious writer could earn a favorable return on the firm's investment no less successfully than an expensive book by a popular author. In *The Book Revolution* Robert Escarpit explains the importance of diversification to reduce publishers' risks: "Fortunately for the trade there is no such thing as a publisher with a single book. In the long run, failures and successes counterbalance one another" (126). Profits offset losses because "the latter are limited in extent, while the former are not" (127).[6] Thus the economic contribution of a minority novel to a firm's profits assured publication of difficult modernist fiction.

A publisher's financial investment did not imply aesthetic or political approval of the books on the firm's list. In practice, however, the major firms interested in fiction were run by people with literary expertise who looked for manuscripts with both literary and commercial value. The publisher was more like a professional than a businessman: "The traditional model of the publisher's role itself crucially depends upon the nineteenth-century emergence of the professional and the businessman as antithetical occupational categories" (Lane 62). The contemporary model of the professional appealed to publishers as well as authors:

> The professional man, it was argued by those who distrusted and feared the ethical implications of the acquisitive aspects of industrialism, thought more of duty than of profit. The gratitude of his client rather than the market defined his reward, and technically he was not paid but granted an *honorarium*. He earned his reputation by discretion, tact and expert knowledge rather than by advertising and financial success. He was a learned man, and his education was broad and comprehensive. Unlike the businessman, who operated within an impersonal market situation, the professional man was involved with his clients at a personal, intimate level. Ideally, he did not have to compete with others of the same profession, at least not to the same extent as the businessman. (Rothblatt 91–92)

While this ideal was never realized, it illuminates the conflict both authors and publishers felt in dealing with the business side of their work.

Even today when conglomerates own many publishing firms, editorial decisions are not based on sales projections alone. In a study of canon-formation in American fiction between 1960 and 1975,

Richard Ohmann notes that editorial decisions were not made by owners but by a "Professional-Managerial class" expressing its own "needs and values" (210). This group had a "conflicted relation to the ruling class" and an "equally mixed relation to the working class" (209). Moreover, books published for aesthetic reasons have been esteemed for their commercial success. Ohmann examines some novels that earned canonical status on several scales and asks how they achieved their position. He concludes: "Canon-formation during this period took place in the interaction between large audiences and gate-keeper intellectuals" (207). Thus the canon omits writers who were merely popular (in this period, Puzo, Wouk, Krantz) as well as those who were merely praised (Coover, Wurlitzer, Sukenick). Instead, it includes writers of bestsellers that also received critical acclaim—Heller, Pynchon, Bellow, Mailer, Roth, Updike, Kesey. Ohmann's research supports Lewes's analysis of the Victorian market: good books do sell, though of course, not all books that sell are good. More important for the minority novel, however, is Ohmann's evidence that avant-garde books which have not sold well enough to enter the canon were nevertheless issued by commercial publishers.[7]

Most studies of publishing blame capitalism for limiting access to the public, but market conditions are congenial to books that appeal to a minority audience. In "The Economics of Publishing, or Adam Smith and Literature," Dan Lacy argues: "Contrary to a general impression, [the media] do not often reflect the personal idiosyncrasies of their owners. . . . Particularly do the economics and technology of the media affect what is widely or massively available to the public. It is true that almost any writer with any trace of perceptible merit can get into print in some way . . ." (408). In contrast to mass media, book publishing is accessible to "almost anyone with a few thousand dollars" (409). After comparing publishing to other media, he concludes:

> The economics of publishing hence permits the issuance of a most wide and varied range of writing, from comic books to the purest expressions of literature, from 25-cent infants' picture books to treatises on the most arcane area of physics, from political tracts to prayerbooks. Its economics also makes publishing exceptionally hospitable to all the winds of political and economic belief and to the

unpopular new forms of literary expression. This is true in part for a reason already pointed out: that anyone may, at relatively little cost, gain access to the national market. (416)

With low production costs, a publisher can remain independent of advertisers or threats of censorship. Specialized audiences provide a sufficient return.

Instead of lamenting the inability of serious writers to become bestsellers, we should compare the aim of seeking a coterie with that of winning a viable public. A coterie can be defined as a readership too small to be justified economically, whereas a minority public is large enough to guarantee a writer continued publication. Although the growth of the reading public has reduced the proportion of the audience interested in serious fiction, as late as the 1930s a sale of only three thousand copies would make a novel a highbrow bestseller, according to Q. D. Leavis in *Fiction and the Reading Public* (47). Indignant that highbrow novels did not achieve the popularity she felt they deserved, Leavis wrote her obituary for serious fiction prematurely because she minimized the importance of a significant minority audience.

Throughout the modernist period, three thousand copies constituted a standard first printing for a novel. A typical contract would call for royalties beginning at 20 percent and rising with sales to 30 percent. On a six-shilling novel, a writer could earn £180, or $900, if the first edition sold out. This provided a reasonable income for the writer as well as an acceptable return for the publisher. Most contracts for first novels stipulated options on the next two manuscripts because publishers expected to expand a writer's market.

A publisher's account of his expenses in 1907 enumerates the financial considerations underlying these contracts. Methuen attempted to persuade Pinker, by then a prominent literary agent, that his client's request for a 30 percent royalty was excessive:

Producing a longish novel	10d.
Advertising, say,	3d.
Author at 30%, about,	1.9 ½ d.
Commission to travellers, say	2d.
Working expenses	2d.
	3.2 ½ d.

> Now, for a 6s. novel the publisher does not receive more than
> 3s.5d.—nearly all the sales being made to libraries and big book sell-
> ers and nearly always at subscription price, i.e. 4s. and 13/12.
> If you deduct 3s.2½d. from 3s.5d. you will see what profit the
> publisher makes when he pays 30%. Excuse this long letter but I dare
> say it will open your eyes. (Pinker Papers, 3 May 1907)

2 ½d. per book was certainly insufficient, but publishers included
contributions to fixed expenses in their costs. Allocation of production costs and working expenses was a subject frequently negotiated
by publisher and agent. By the time a contract was signed, both
expected to earn enough on three thousand copies to continue to
operate. John Feather points out that the author was the "supplier"
of a "product": "The supplier needed his profits, just as the producer
needed his, and it was unreasonable to expect regular supplies of
acceptable goods unless the supplier was adequately and regularly
recompensed for his work" (179). Publishers found that with a limited investment a small edition of a minority novel could pay its way,
and if acclaim sustained sales, profits might soar.[8] In 1910 John
Murray explained the value of a publisher's investment: "Novels
nowadays have a very short life until an author has reached a success measured by a 10,000 sale. Only after that does there seem to
be a continuous sale for previous works by the same author" (Pinker
Papers, 24 February 1910). Serious fiction was not a bad risk.

Conrad, Joyce, and Lawrence were desirable authors to publishers because there was a reliable market for books expected to sell
steadily to a minority public. Their careers followed a similar pattern.
Publishers accepted their first manuscripts immediately and made
editorial suggestions. As novices, all three writers appreciated this
advice. Editors rarely made specific demands, but they provided an
early response for the author's consideration. Between acceptance
and publication, extensive revision improved their early work.
Editors expected the new fiction to penetrate the highbrow market
and eventually reach a wide public. In time, their judgment proved
accurate.

In contrast to Victorian novelists, however, modernists' initial
willingness to serve an apprenticeship ended when they failed to
attract the audience they sought. Having based their rhetorical decisions on conceptions of readers partly formed by publishers' advice,

modernists lost confidence in their advisors when the public did not respond as predicted. Conrad increasingly relied on his own judgment, and Joyce and Lawrence, in their disappointment, blamed publishers for blocking access to the public. Unable to reconcile their desire for popularity with an aesthetic hostile to popular taste, Joyce and Lawrence made publishers scapegoats.[9] Although it was primarily libel and obscenity that forced editors to demand deletions, Joyce and Lawrence were caught in an ideological trap that made any revision to expedite publication seem a betrayal of art for money. Every editorial suggestion was suspect because its purpose might be to increase sales rather than to improve aesthetic form. Despite authors' recalcitrance, editors were so eager to publish the new controversial fiction that they urged Joyce and Lawrence to remove actionable passages. Neither would comply. Acrimonious negotiations caused both writers to charge that publishers were philistines whose avarice blinded them to art.

When commercial publishers demanded revisions, the reasons were legal, not financial, though the two were connected. For example, Grant Richards objected to *Dubliners* only when his printer refused to set type. In response to Joyce's intransigence in refusing to delete the word "bloody" from "Grace," Grant Richards mocked his impracticality: "If I had written your stories I should certainly wish to be able to afford your attitude" (Ellmann 221). Abandoning commercial publishers, Joyce and Lawrence won the artistic freedom they sought, but at a high price: they lost the editorial advice that ordinarily mediated between writers and the reading public.[10]

Although publishers like Grant Richards expected modernist writers to cooperate in removing legal obstacles, the emergence of private presses made cooperation unnecessary. Private publishers emerge as heroes in biographies of Joyce and Lawrence, but these patrons lacked the expertise of professional editors. In *Published in Paris,* a history of expatriate private presses between the world wars, Hugh Ford corrects exaggerated estimates of patrons' literary perspicacity. They wanted to participate in the avant-garde, but like commercial publishers, owners of private presses also had financial objectives. Untouched by the restraints of British and American censorship, private presses enjoyed a profitable trade in banned books. Sharing writers' desire to defy conventions, patrons dispensed sympathy but not the editorial support commercial firms could provide. Often in awe of their authors, private publishers were unwilling and unqualified to give literary advice. Worthwhile manuscripts rarely languished in neglect. Instead, private presses rescued books of uncertain merit from the oblivion they may have deserved. For example, Ford points out that Robert McAlmon, whose wife, Bryher, financed Contact Editions, "could afford to publish his own books after they had been rejected by commercial publishers. He could do it without changing a word" (Ford 94). Nor was it necessary to own a press to be published. In 1929 Jack Kahane announced the Obelisk Press "was prepared to publish in Paris, 'within a month,' any book of 'literary merit' which had been banned in England" (Ford 352). Despite this open offer, none of the "cafe geniuses" who complained that no publisher was "broadminded enough to understand their aspirations" submitted suppressed manuscripts (Ford 354). Commercial firms published books of great and meager literary value, and the novels that raised legal obstacles eventually overcame censorship thanks to commercial firms' willingness to defend them in court.

In the key legal decisions that eventually permitted *Ulysses* and *Lady Chatterley's Lover* to be sold openly, the period's ideological contradictions control the arguments. Commercial publishers could not issue work that was illegal, yet they knew that erotic fiction would be extremely profitable. Publishers eventually defended this fiction in court on the grounds that it was not erotic, but they wanted to publish it because it was.[11] They persuaded the courts to accept the argument that artistic necessity justified obscenity. In both cases, judicial opinions inadvertently parodied the "art for art's sake" slogan in their recurring description of pornography as "dirt for dirt's sake." In practice, the distinction between art and dirt often depended on the perceived audience. Throughout the nineteenth century, prosecutors tended to seize material only when it addressed "persons with incomes of less than £500 a year. The law was not invoked against the authors of serious literature nor the morals of the better-off members of the community" (Hyde 1–2).

As moral standards became stricter in the Victorian period, courts were asked to establish a new consensus on the meaning of obscenity, but judicial opinions reflected the ideological conflict between art and money. While defendants invoked the purity of their intentions, prosecutors emphasized the work's rhetorical effect, and they assumed this effect would vary with the social class of the reader. An 1867 decision included a test generally accepted as a statement of English common law:

> Whether the tendency of the matter charged as obscenity is to deprave and corrupt those whose minds are open to such immoral influences and into whose hands a publication of this sort may fall. (Hyde 3)

This test protected Thomas Hardy and George Moore from prosecution, though they experienced unofficial censorship by the circulating libraries. Applying this standard, the courts banned Frank Harris's autobiography *My Life and Loves* (1922) as well as Radclyffe Hall's *The Well of Loneliness,* published by Jonathan Cape in 1928. Although the literary merit of *Well of Loneliness* was recognized, and its most explicit passage was "that night they were not divided," it was considered obscene because its subject, however chastely described, was a lesbian relationship (Hyde 4). It was not republished until 1948, when its appearance was not contested. In the intervening years, authors' artistic intentions had become a successful defense against obscenity.

Although its difficulty stipulated an elite audience, modernist fiction violated moral standards too flagrantly to be ignored. Even the briefs for the defense did not dispute the obscenity of certain passages in *Ulysses* and *Lady Chatterley's Lover.* Instead, they argued that the author's intention and the effect of the work as a whole had to be considered. Both sides regarded high sales as evidence of pornography, but the defense assured the court these books were too difficult to be popular or profitable.

Ruling on *Ulysses* in 1933, Justice John M. Woolsey analyzed both authorial intention and rhetorical effect. The text passed the first test because Joyce's intent was not "dirt for dirt's sake" (Woolsey x):

> [H]is attempt sincerely and honestly to realize his objective has required him incidentally to use certain words which are generally considered dirty words and has led at times to what many think is a

too poignant preoccupation with sex in the thoughts of his characters. (Woolsey ix–x)

Woolsey exonerated Joyce on the grounds that his intention had
been to describe "persons of the lower middle class living in Dublin
in 1904" (Woolsey ix). Thus, if the "theme of sex" recurs in their
minds, "it must always be remembered that his locale was Celtic and
his season Spring" (Woolsey x). Underlying Woolsey's opinion was
the assumption that highbrow readers would consider vulgar language suitable to lower-middle-class subjects. He allowed mimetic
realism to justify any obscenity in the novel.

Applying the second test, he cited the legal standard of obscenity: "tending to stir the sex impulses or to lead to sexually impure and
lustful thoughts" (Woolsey xi). His task, as he defined it, was to consider the book's "effect on a person with average sex instincts—what
the French would call *l'homme moyen sensuel*" (Woolsey xi), that is,
a person such as himself. Woolsey said he found the book too difficult and too disgusting to produce any erotic response: "the effect of
'Ulysses' on the reader undoubtedly is somewhat emetic, nowhere
does it tend to be an aphrodisiac" (Woolsey xii). To be sure he was
correct, he devised a test he considered valid: he consulted two of his
friends, and they agreed with him. Difficulty was not only a sign of
art, but it was also a barrier to illicit pleasure. As the defense attor-
neys had argued, "It is axiomatic that only what is understandable can
corrupt" (Moscato 258). If *Ulysses* had been addressed to a wider
audience, Joyce would have been guilty of "exploiting obscenity" to
increase sales (Woolsey ix). In aligning pornography and readability
against art and difficulty, Woolsey enforced the modernist ideology
that art and money were antithetical. As long as erotic fiction
addressed an elite audience, it could be defended as art.

The issue of audience was raised in the appeal filed a year later.
Although Woolsey's decision was upheld, the dissenting opinion
written by Justice Martin T. Manton proposed different tests. He
argued that obscenity statutes applied to particular passages rather
than to the work as a whole, and he dealt with the effect of such passages on the most vulnerable segment of the community rather than
on average or elite members. Since the presence of obscene passages

had not been disputed, Manton addressed intent and effect. He rejected artistic intention as a defense, because any pornographer could claim that he saw nothing obscene in his own product (Moscato 458). The relevant issue for Manton was the effect of obscenity on the "young and inexperienced" whom the law sought to protect, not on "those who pose as the more highly developed and intelligent" (Moscato 459, 461).

Manton insisted that obscenity laws were not written to serve literary interests:

> The people do not exist for the sake of literature; to give the author fame, the publisher wealth, and the book a market. On the contrary, literature exists for the sake of the people. . . . Art for art's sake is heartless and soon grows artless; art for the public market is not art at all, but commerce; art for the people's service is a noble, vital, and permanent element of human life. (Moscato 461)

Although Manton believed art should improve rather than imitate life, both he and Woolsey accepted the dichotomy of art and money. While Woolsey concurred with the defense's blandishments that the difficulty of art blocked any "aphrodisiac" response, Manton correctly estimated the market value of modernist fiction in spite of its difficulty. *Ulysses* was in demand as soon as it was banned. When Sylvia Beach's 1922 edition appeared, there were not enough copies to meet the demand. A second edition of two thousand copies sold out in four days, and another pirated edition printed in monthly installments sold forty thousand copies a month (*Selected Letters* 292, 315). Joyce helplessly watched pirated editions reap his profits.

Woolsey's decision became an important precedent in obscenity cases, but *Lady Chatterley's Lover* had to wait more than twenty years to benefit from it. In 1959 Grove Press sued to publish the first legal unexpurgated edition. Like Woolsey, Federal Judge Frederick Bryan found that Lawrence's purpose was not prurient: "Thus, this is an honest and sincere novel of literary merit and its dominant theme and effect, taken as a whole, is not an appeal to the prurient interest of the average reader" (Hyde 13). He judged the "passages describing sexual intercourse and using phallic language" to be "necessary to Lawrence's development of plot, theme, and character"

(Squires 201). Evaluating the book's effect on readers, he tried to determine "whether to the average person, applying contemporary community standards, the dominant theme of the [novel] taken as a whole appeals to prurient interest" (Squires 201). Like Woolsey, he found that the book was not "dirt for dirt's sake" (Hyde 13).

In addition to these tests, Bryan explicitly considered the way the book was marketed as a way to assess its effect: "A work of literature published and distributed through normal channels by a reputable publisher stands on quite a different footing from hard core pornography furtively sold for the purpose of profiting by the titillation of the dirty-minded" (Hyde 13). Since it was written as art and sold as art, the novel was declared not to be obscene. Persuaded that aesthetic value outweighed erotic appeal, Bryan also reinforced the dichotomy between art and money. The novel's aesthetic value must have been great indeed, because this edition sold 3,225,000 copies in the first eight months (Meyers 387).

Hardly anyone calls this fiction obscene today, but Joyce thought *Lady Chatterley* "a piece of propaganda in favour of something which, outside D. H. L.'s country at any rate, makes all the propaganda for itself," and Lawrence considered *Ulysses* "the dirtiest, most indecent, obscene thing ever written" (Meyers 362). The testimony of Joyce, Lawrence, and more than three million readers suggests these books were not merely the aesthetic objects publishers' lawyers claimed. Obscenity had a powerful rhetorical effect and a predictable economic value.

The mutual effort of authors and publishers to exploit the commercial value of this fiction without admitting mercenary motives vexed their negotiations. Lawrence's publishing experiences illustrate how modernists used obscenity as a weapon against social conventions, defending it as art, while they profited from it. His correspondence with publishers also demonstrates that they were interested in avant-garde fiction partly because of its erotic content. From the beginning of his career, the eroticism of Lawrence's fiction attracted and frightened publishers, but contradictory ideologies of authorship dictated the terms of Lawrence's responses to editors' requests for revisions.

Just as writers wanted to escape literary conventions, segments of the public supported the new fiction to distinguish themselves from the popular audience. Difficulty, paradoxically, contributed to the popularity of modernist writing by attracting readers eager to be associated with an avant-garde. As modernists became more recondite, the public pursued them more avidly. Lawrence and Joyce became celebrities. Robert McAlmon described the blind adulation Joyce received when he gave a reading of "Anna Livia Plurabelle" in Paris: "But they had set their faces into what they believed the proper expression for listening, and it was cruel to ask them to crack the wax or break the mask with a natural grin. Holy, holy, holy—and not one of them got more out of that reading than I did, and I had read the passage, indeed, Joyce had once read it to me himself" (314). McAlmon, who appreciated Joyce's talent, aimed his satire not at Joyce but at Joyce's fans.

A closer look at each writer's publishing experiences can correct the simplifications we have inherited. Commercial publishers accepted the first manuscripts of modernist writers and were prepared to support their subsequent work. The editorial objections that did occur focused on libel and obscenity rather than on formal complexity or social criticism. In contrast to the typical relationship between author and publisher at the turn of the century, however, modernist writers refused to make the revisions publishers requested because they equated revision with capitulation. Although Conrad, Joyce, and Lawrence had varied disputes with publishers, the rhetorical skepticism each expressed at some point in his career was not his attitude when he became a writer, nor when he wrote his major books. The early publishing experiences of modernist writers were more typical of commercially successful novelists than they or their partisans admitted. Modernist writers did not ignore readers; commercial publishers did not ignore modernist writers. The relationship between them was more complicated than either myth suggests.

The answer to the question "Who paid for modernism?" is "people with money," but in this period money was available from sources other than commercial firms. Private fortunes, the culture of the avant-garde, and cheap printing methods made it possible for individual patrons to become publishers. Although they lacked the literary expertise of professional editors, private publishers were in a position to finance modernists' opposition to popular culture. In another sense, the answer to the question is that writers themselves paid dearly by losing the feedback editors, reviewers, and readers normally provided, as well as the income commercial firms were capable of generating. Modernists' editorial freedom contributed to their successes as well as their excesses; it is time to recognize both.

CHAPTER TWO

Joseph Conrad: Sincerity and Solidarity

A choice between literary quality and popularity was unthinkable for Joseph Conrad when he embarked on his writing career. Late Victorian writers and publishers shared a desire for high sales. A pragmatic compromise between art as a sacred calling and publishing as a profitable business satisfied both parties. Conrad's desire for popularity was an artistic compulsion as much as a financial necessity. His literary agent, J. B. Pinker, who also served Joyce and Lawrence briefly, considered Conrad's attitude exemplary. Pinker classified Conrad, Henry James, and George Gissing together as model clients: "Of the writers I have known intimately, the three greatest . . . have always in my experience felt and frankly discussed a desire to meet the public taste, and to win popularity, and all the best men of my acquaintance have been keenly anxious that their work should be made to produce as much money as possible" (Hepburn 192, 193n). Conrad, like Joyce and Lawrence early in their careers, believed economic success rewarded artistic achievement.

The example of late Victorian novelists who pleased both the public and the critics made these goals seem attainable. Assessing the balance between popularity and literary value in 1898, Conrad dismissed writers who were merely popular:

> The *Woman Who Did* had a kind of success, of curiosity mostly and
> that only amongst the philistines—the sort of people who read Marie
> Corelli and Hall Caine. Neither of these writers belongs to literature.
> All three are very popular with the public—and they are also puffed
> in the press. There are no lasting qualities in their work. . . . They are
> popular because they express the common thought, and the common
> man is delighted to find himself in accord with people he supposes
> distinguished. (*Letters* 2:137)

Conrad proceeded to contrast such writers with those he admired:
Rudyard Kipling, J. M. Barrie, George Meredith, Turgenev, George
Moore, T. Watts-Dunton, and H. G. Wells—authors who were both
critically acclaimed and popular. Although Conrad was contemptuous of the popular audience, he also dreaded writing for a coterie.
He believed "lasting qualities" would produce both critical recognition and a livelihood. As Ian Watt argues, Conrad was a transitional
figure at the turn of the century who benefited from his Victorian
expectations of the audience:

> Conrad belonged to no coterie; he seems to have had no interest in
> experiment for its own sake; and in his fiction, far from flaunting his
> differences in taste and attitude from mankind at large, he often
> attempted to appear more affirmative and conformist than he really
> was. There were, no doubt, many motives underlying this attempt,
> including Conrad's economic need to widen his circle of readers; and
> the wish to be popular certainly had some adverse effects on Conrad's
> writing. At the same time, it was precisely because he attempted to
> write for a larger audience, and steadily kept his distance from the
> *avant garde* in its hot pursuit of literary, social, and ethical innovation,
> that Conrad was able to express the problems of his own time and of
> ours with a much more inclusive and penetrating understanding than
> his contemporaries. (Watt 359)

Conrad aspired to the consistent productivity of the professional.
He did not regard writing as inevitably unreliable; he usually blamed
himself for his writing blocks, seeing them as character defects.
Conrad tried to approach writing in a workmanlike way. He knew
the value of skill and steadiness—traits esteemed by his period but
rarely associated with genius. He distanced himself from the
Romantic image of the artist: "I own to a, not I hope very peculiar,
dislike of falling, even by the remotest appearance, into the class of

those disorderly talents whose bohemianism, irregularity and general irresponsibility of conduct are neither in my tradition and my training nor in my character" (*Letters* 3:248–49). His view of work as an expression of spiritual value, of fidelity itself, owed as much to the bourgeois tenor of the period as to Flaubert's claims for the artist as craftsman.

In their emphasis on the psychological sources of Conrad's art, however, most of his biographers minimize the importance of his rhetorical aims. Their narratives attempt to convey his uniqueness, his suffering, and his unconscious motives. Frederick Karl's *Three Lives* illustrates the hegemony of the myth of the martyred artist found in many biographies. In contrast to Karl's psychological portrait, Conrad's letters are like snapshots that capture him in a variety of inconsistent moods. In some, he is Karl's creator, powerless before his imagination, but in others he is a conscious craftsman practicing his skills.[1] Many of his letters articulate the professional concerns that also affected his fiction. Complicating interpretation, Conrad often disparaged his work when he felt proud of it to avoid seeming boastful.[2] He flattered his correspondents. He longed for money when he was poor, and he depreciated it when he was rich.

Karl's account of Conrad's attitude to his audience in 1896 reflects the anti-rhetorical emphasis of the model of the author as artist: "Conrad's contempt for his audience was constant for the next fifteen years at least, and he gained considerable satisfaction from the fact that the average man would have no idea what he, the author, was striving for. Yet, at the same time, he desperately wanted that average man to buy his book. In this respect, Conrad followed that detestation of the bourgeoisie—who, after all, bought the books— which began with Flaubert and continued into the modernist movement" (385–86).

In his letters, however, ambivalence rather than contempt characterizes Conrad's attitude to his reader. Early in his career Conrad felt he depended on inspiration to compensate for his ignorance of the public and his lack of craftsmanship, but with experience, he considered erratic control of his work a sign of ineptitude. He modified his methods of achieving his aesthetic and rhetorical aims when his publishing experiences changed his conception of his readers. To account for the development of Conrad's fiction, the rhetorical circuit linking him to his readers is as important as psychological factors. Between the poles of helplessness and mastery hovered his ideal of the serious writer committed to mediating between inner vision and audience response.

The ideological antithesis between art and money permeates Karl's defense of Conrad's artistic integrity throughout his career: since Conrad's "reputation depends on the words he writes, he does not wish to write idly something that may injure that reputation. This consciousness of his worth apart from the marketplace suggests he had not forsaken the role of serious artist . . ." (772). For Karl, concern with sales necessarily compromises art. But Conrad's concern with reputation was not always opposed to the marketplace, nor was his interest in the market opposed to art.

Karl regards Conrad's professionalism as a betrayal of art: "Since he was professional enough to throw off fiction that was no longer dependent on memory, he could have played the more popular markets for easy money, or else turned out articles and essays on his past, a more popular follow-up to his reminiscences, vignettes of Poland and France and the like" (735). Karl belittles professionalism by associating it with popular markets and high sales ("easy money") as well as autobiographical narratives. In contrast, he links art to writing rooted not just in memory—reminiscences obviously draw on memory—but to the expression of unconscious memories. He argues that Conrad remained a driven, and therefore superior, writer to the end of his career.

Karl uses the correlation between Conrad's frequent illnesses and his most productive periods as evidence of the unconscious sources of his fiction. He argues that Conrad needed to induce the threat of disaster to work at all: "This accumulation of anxieties, worries, fears, and assorted guilt feelings was connected, evidently, to his way of working and to the functioning of his literary imagination. Apparently, he could not work effectively unless he were close to breakdown, on the edge of psychic disorders, ill in body and mind" (527). This pattern reached its climax in 1903: "With the early work on *Nostromo*, Conrad's greatest achievement, we have a sense of epic labors, the pained and disturbed artist turning out copy at an agonizingly slow rate, while burning within with a raging self-hatred" (528). While Karl concludes that these states of near hysteria demonstrate intense introspection, they also suggest the rhetorical anxiety of the professional. In addition to self-exposure, Conrad dreaded critical and commercial failure.

Both Conrad and contemporary critics respected his desire for a large audience as long as sales were low; commercial failure merely confirmed the philistine taste of the mass audience. When *Chance* became a bestseller in 1913, however, critics interpreted his new-found popular success as the sign of a sudden sell-out. Certainly Conrad wanted to sell his books, but his motives were not entirely economic. He also wanted the "average man" to understand what he was striving for and shaped his fiction with his reader in mind. Conrad recognized the obstacles he faced. As he wrote a friend while working on *The Nigger of the "Narcissus,"* "one writes only half the book; the other half is with the reader" (*Letters* 1:370). Despite his awareness of the difficulty, if not the impossibility, of being understood, he could not relinquish this goal. Whereas modernists like Joyce made their texts difficult, forcing the reader to participate in writing "the other half," Conrad was so appalled by the gulf between all writers and all readers that he steadily tried to make his fiction more accessible to help the reader meet him halfway.

Conrad also made the themes of fidelity and solidarity, being true to oneself and true to others, as central to his life as to his fiction. Fidelity demanded a Romantic sincerity, keeping faith with his subjective self; solidarity required a connection to a community. He found that solidarity was a more difficult objective than sincerity. As he wrote in 1892: "One quickly gets to know oneself. The difficulty comes in knowing others" (*Letters* 1:119). In contrast to Victorian novelists' intimate relationship with readers, late-nineteenth-century subjectivist epistemology blocked the passage from sincerity to solidarity.[3] No matter how faithfully he rendered his vision, no matter how scrupulously he tried to make the reader see as he did, subjectivism limited communication.

Beyond knowing oneself and others, as a writer Conrad had to convey his knowledge to a reader. In 1895 he doubted that one could communicate with any reader: "No man's light is good to any of his fellows. That's my creed—from beginning to end. Thats [*sic*] my view of life—a view that rejects all formulas dogmas and principles of other people's making. These are only a web of illusions. We are too varied. Another man's truth is only a dismal lie to me. . . . You can see now how little anything I may say is worth to anybody" (*Letters* 1:253). Although comparable skepticism led other modernist writers to forms as idiosyncratic as subjective knowledge, Conrad tried to compensate by expressing his vision as comprehensibly as possible.

To know his audience better, Conrad turned to publishers for advice. His first submission, *Almayer's Folly*, led him to Edward Garnett, then a reader for T. Fisher Unwin. Unwin's nephew described the typical path of an unsolicited manuscript through readers to his uncle: "The 'discoveries' were Edward Garnett's and W. H. Chesson's, but to T. Fisher Unwin must be given the credit both for employing them and acting upon their advice. . . . T. F. U. always believed that if a book had quality it would make its way, whether the author was known or not" (Unwin 80). Conrad's work impressed both readers, and Unwin confirmed their judgment with an offer.

Conrad's report of his first meeting with Garnett portrays the publisher's reader as middleman between art and money. Assuming a tone of mockery, Conrad wrote his aunt:

> "We are paying you very little," he told me, "but, remember, dear Sir, that you are unknown and your book will appeal to a very limited public. Then there is the question of taste. Will the public like it? We are risking something also. We are publishing you in a handsome volume at six shillings, and you know that whatever we bring out always receives serious critical attention in the literary journals. . . . Write something shorter—same type of thing—for our Pseudonym Library, and if it suits us, we shall be very happy to be able to give you a much better cheque." (*Letters* 1:180)

Despite the tone and the exaggeration (he never wrote for the Pseudonym Library market), Conrad explains the economics of publishing accurately.

Garnett's version of their meeting emphasizes Conrad's willingness to defer to the editor's professional opinion. Garnett recalled that when he read a draft of *Almayer's Folly*, he was "enthralled by the strange atmosphere and poetic vision," but he criticized the characterization of Willems (Garnett 8). Conrad welcomed his suggestions and revised several passages accordingly. Although Garnett represented the publisher, Conrad had to remind Garnett that sales were as important to him as art. Garnett assured Conrad it was a "necessity for a writer to follow his own path and disregard the public's taste." Conrad, however, disdained such idealism: "I *won't* live in an attic!" (Garnett 9). This anecdote illustrates a sympathy for artists typical of editors and publishers. Garnett, who represented the publisher's interests, idealized the independence the writer enjoyed, but Conrad, the artist, wanted a secure place in society.

Garnett's support and advice were crucial to Conrad's literary development. Conrad's letters from 1895 to 1899 abound with praise, gratitude, and dependence. Even discounting much of this as flattery, one feels Conrad's indebtedness. Mentor, critic, agent, conscience—Garnett was all these. In Garnett, Conrad found an ideal reader: "To be read—as you do me the honour to read me—is an ideal experience—and the experience of an ideal" (*Letters* 1:205). Eager for Garnett's comments, Conrad besieged him for criticism and praise. When the former came, he chafed but usually followed Garnett's suggestions. When the latter arrived, Conrad waxed ecstatic and begged for reassurance that the compliments were sincere.

As Conrad's "ideal" reader, Garnett helped him learn how to reach the ordinary reader: "Am I mindful enough of Your teaching—of Your expoundings of the ways of the reader?" (*Letters* 1:273). Garnett never told Conrad what to write. His role as first reader was to articulate a response. Passages that were unclear, inconsistent, unconvincing, or tedious might be identified, but any rewriting was Conrad's. To encourage Conrad, Garnett assured him *Almayer's Folly* was both good and likely to be popular: "I think it will strike the Public too (the great gross Public that you accuse me of knowing!) as very interesting and very fresh" (Garnett 19).

Conrad sought Garnett's advice to advance his career, certainly, but he did not see his desire to reach an audience as a betrayal of his art. He respected Garnett's integrity too much to suspect him of serving the publisher's interest in place of the author's. He was eager to revise his work to incorporate Garnett's literary and commercial advice because he felt it would improve his books. Working with Garnett, Conrad learned that sincere expression of sincere impressions did not necessarily convince the reader; readers' responses were difficult to control. Despite George Henry Lewes's confidence in the value of sincerity, this Romantic emphasis on the writer's state of mind did not satisfy Conrad's sense of the professional's responsibility to the reader.

When Conrad could not please Garnett, however, he invoked Romantic ideas of the spontaneous origin of art to justify himself. He protested that he could not rewrite the twenty-fourth chapter of *An Outcast of the Islands,* though he saw its faults: "Nothing now can unmake my mistake. I shall try—but I shall try without faith, because all my work is produced unconsciously (so to speak) and I cannot meddle to any purpose with what is within myself—I am sure you understand what I mean.—It isn't in me to improve what has got itself written.—" (*Letters* 1:246). Attributing his work to an unconscious source, Conrad tried to mitigate his failure. Although this passage resembles other modernists' reasons for refusing to alter their work to suit critics, it was not Conrad's final word. His next paragraph begins, "Still with your help I may try. All the paragraphs marked by You to that effect shall be cut out."

The initial problem was not that Garnett callously forced Conrad to alter his work to suit the reader, but that Conrad could not cast his vision in a form that would produce the effect he sought on the reader. Conrad expressed his dissatisfaction with this manuscript in terms of his failure to achieve the rhetorical effect he intended: "I had some hazy idea that in the first part I would present to the reader the impression of the sea—the ship—the seamen. But I doubt having conveyed anything but the picture of my own folly.—I doubt the sincerity of my own impressions" (*Letters* 1:287). Here Conrad explicitly connected sincerity and solidarity. To prove the sincerity of his impressions, he had to be able to communicate them. Sincerity could only be measured by the rhetorical success of producing an impression of sincerity on the reader; the reader's judgment validated the writer's authenticity.

Conrad also used Flaubert's defense, which equated the value of the artist's work with the amount of labor expended, when he needed an excuse. Urging Unwin to get as much as possible for serial rights, Conrad first defended the sincerity of the work and then asked to be compensated for the difficulty of producing it:

> Bad or good I cannot be ashamed of what is produced in perfect single mindedness—I cannot be ashamed of those things that are like fragments of my innermost being produced for the public gaze.
>
> But I must live. I don't care much where I appear since the acceptance of such stories is not based upon their artistic worth. . . . And if you knew the wear and tear of my writing you would understand my desire for some return. (*Letters* 1:293)

Buttressing Romantic self-exposure with Flaubertian wear and tear, this plea must be set against his cynical estimate only a year later of someone else's attempt to use it: "But it comes to this, if his point of view is accepted, that having suffered is sufficient excuse for the production of rubbish. Well! It may be true too. I may yet make my profit of that argument" (*Letters* 1:395). These inconsistent attitudes indicate the impact of competing ideologies of authorship on Conrad at the time.

As a professional author, Conrad was able to assess his prospects accurately. He realized the fragmentation of the reading public created several markets. Analyzing his position in 1898, he distinguished his own viable public from both a wide audience and a coterie:

> I have some—literary—reputation but the future is anything but certain, for I am not a popular author and probably I never shall be. That does not sadden me at all, for I have never had the ambition to write for the all-powerful masses. I haven't the taste for democracy—and democracy hasn't the taste for me. I have gained the appreciation of a few select spirits and I do not doubt I shall be able to create a public for myself, limited it is true, but one which will permit me to earn my bread. I do not dream of fortune; besides, one does not find it in an inkwell. But I confess to you I dream of peace, a little reputation, and the rest of my life devoted to the service of Art and free from material worries. (*Letters* 1:390)

He longed to devote his life to "Art," but he had to earn a living, and he understood how to work in the literary marketplace.

Despite this realistic assessment, he yearned for the fame and fortune his predecessors had achieved:

> Now, note the inconsequence of the human animal: I want to rush into print whereby my sentimentalism, my incorrect attitude to life—all I wish to hide in the wilds of Essex—shall be disclosed to the public gaze! Do I do it for money? Chi lo sà! Perhaps. Or no!—it would be too indecent. I am in a bad way. Now if I could only attain to become (is that English?) . . . a minor Thackeray decency would be preserved and shekels gathered at the same time. (*Letters* 1:347)

Contrasting himself with Thackeray, Conrad articulates the modernist dilemma of authorship. Although Thackeray could preserve his aesthetic integrity and gather shekels at the same time, Conrad felt that he had to choose between them.

Conrad could attract a discriminating public, but he sought payment on a scale only a few popular novelists justified. The growth of a market for romance, mystery, adventure, and escape novels made so many inferior writers rich that Conrad and others with higher standards felt underpaid. Although modernist writers defined their art in opposition to popular fiction, they nevertheless believed that artists deserved to be rewarded. As much as they disdained this equation of aesthetic worth and market value, it crept into their attitude toward readers. Instead of writing for the literate minority audience and accepting the income it provided, many modernists raged at the public for ignoring them, and many increasingly wrote for themselves rather than any audience. Conrad took another route. Fearing solipsism and dreading a coterie audience, he tried to imagine particular readers.

In addition to the professional question of craftsmanship and the practical question of earning a living, an audience was essential to Conrad's aesthetic goals. Two famous prefaces bracketing his career expound Conrad's rhetorical intentions. In both the 1897 preface to *The Nigger of the "Narcissus"* and the 1920 preface to *Chance*, he states his conception of the artist's relation to society. In 1897 he announced: "My task which I am trying to achieve is, by the power of the written word to make you hear, to make you feel—it is, before all, to make you *see*" (*Nigger* 14). His editor persuaded him to delete an even more emphatic statement of his desire to communicate with his reader: "And, after all, everyone desires to be understood" (*Letters* 1:377n). Conrad connected this rhetorical aim to the Romantic conviction that sincerity could achieve solidarity:

> In a single-minded attempt of that kind, if one be deserving and fortunate, one may perchance attain to such clearness of sincerity that at last the presented vision of regret or pity, of terror or mirth, shall awaken in the hearts of the beholders that feeling of unavoidable solidarity . . . which binds men to each other and all mankind to the visible world. (*Nigger* 14–15)

Conrad included a practical test in his Romantic assertions. He measured the sincerity of his impressions by his rhetorical success in producing an impression of sincerity on the reader. The alternative view that the writer's sincerity alone guaranteed the quality of his work too easily justified the kind of writing that Conrad's pride in his craft made him disdain.

Although Garnett embodied Conrad's sense of his audience in the years of his apprenticeship, a turning point came when Conrad was writing *The Nigger of the "Narcissus."* Still confessing his doubts to Garnett, Conrad introduced a new tone of intransigence which he reinforced by gradually sending Garnett less copy. At the end of 1896, he wrote his editor: "It is as if I had broken with my conscience, quarreled with the inward voice" (*Letters* 1:321). But he followed this apology with an assertion of confidence in his new work: "Of course nothing can alter the course of the 'Nigger'. Let it be unpopularity if it *must* be. But it seems to me that the thing—precious as it is to me—is trivial enough on the surface to have some charms for the man in the street. As to lack of incident, well—it's life" (*Letters* 1:321). Still concerned with the "man in the street," he defended his own judgment. He answered Garnett's warnings with confidence in his work's appeal.

After publishing his first books with Unwin, Conrad had so much confidence in the manuscript of *Nigger of the "Narcissus"* that he asked for twice as much as he had been paid before. Having published Conrad's previous books at a loss, Unwin balked. Booksellers bought all eleven hundred copies of the first edition of *Almayer's Folly*, but despite favorable reviews, the books sold slowly. Nevertheless, Unwin continued to back his judgment with money. He published Conrad's next book, *An Outcast of the Islands*, and wanted to buy *Nigger of the "Narcissus"* as well.[4] Conrad decided to respond to an inquiry he had received from Smith, Elder, and Company, but their offer was no better than Unwin's. Urging Conrad to seek another publisher or an agent, Garnett advised Conrad to submit the new book to William Heinemann and Company. Here Garnett acted as Conrad's friend and agent rather than Unwin's employee. Besides editing the manuscript, Garnett persuaded Sidney Pawling to accept *Nigger* for Heinemann and got William Blackwood to publish it serially in *Blackwood's Magazine*. Gratefully, Conrad wrote Garnett: "You sent me to Pawling—You sent me to Blackwoods—when are you going to send me to heaven?" (*Letters* 1:378). In addition to offering better terms than Unwin for *Nigger*, Pawling sold the still pending serial rights of "The Rescue" to S. S. McClure in New York for the respectable sum of £250 (*Letters* 2:44).

Unwin proposed publishing *Tales of Unrest* to capitalize on the success of *Nigger*. Conrad was outraged that Unwin might injure Heinemann's sales. He ignored the fact that if Unwin had published both books, no conflict would have occurred. Instead, Conrad slandered Unwin: "The man is unsafe and I am a fool when dealing with such a type for I can't understand it" (Karl 415). He asked Unwin to delay publication, and Unwin agreed to wait. Despite losses on earlier books, Conrad's defection to Heinemann, and the burden of trying to sell short stories instead of a novel, Unwin cooperated fully. His reward was Conrad's self-righteous indignation at the publisher's materialism. From Unwin's point of view, his investment in Conrad's early, unprofitable books was lost when Conrad decided to leave him at the first sign of a better offer. Seeing the early promise in *Almayer's Folly* and *An Outcast of the Islands,* Unwin had both commercial and aesthetic reasons to continue to support Conrad, though not as lavishly as Conrad expected.

When strong critical acclaim for *Nigger of the "Narcissus"* failed to generate commensurate sales, Conrad's initial rhetorical position faltered. His conception of his audience contracted. Telling a friend about the reviews of *Nigger,* he described his rhetorical dilemma at the end of 1897: "When writing one thinks of half-a-dozen (at least I do) men or so—and if these are satisfied and take the trouble to say it in so many words then no writer deserves a more splendid recompense. On the other hand there is the problem of the daily bread which can not be solved by praise—public or private" (*Letters* 1:434). Painfully aware of a dearth of readers, Conrad made two important rhetorical decisions. He narrowed his target audience to a particular group embodied in the readership of *Blackwood's Magazine* (or "Maga"), and he introduced Marlow as a narrator in "Youth."

Close relationships with Blackwood and one of his editors, David Meldrum, helped Conrad sustain a particular conception of his readers. After buying the serial rights to *Nigger of the "Narcissus,"* Blackwood replaced Garnett as Conrad's practical and ideal audience. The reputation of "Maga" persuaded Conrad that its readers would understand him. Characterizing the magazine as "conservative and masculine," Ian Watt argues that Conrad was now able to imagine himself speaking to an audience responsive to Marlow's "bluff heartiness." As Conrad recalled in 1911, "One was in decent company there and had a good sort of public. There isn't a single club and messroom and man-of-war in the British Seas and Dominions which hasn't its copy of Maga" (Watt 131–32). The public Conrad stipulated for himself resembled Marlow's audience aboard the *Nellie:* men who managed the empire (Menand 107). Conrad's most prolific period followed. From 1898 to 1904 he wrote "Youth," "Heart of Darkness," *Lord Jim,* and *Nostromo.* In addition, he drafted an early version of *Chance,* while collaborating with Ford Madox Hueffer (later Ford Madox Ford) on *The Inheritors* and *Romance.*

Apart from the rhetorical benefits Marlow provides, Karl accounts for the fecundity of this period in Conrad's career psychologically: "Remarkable about this five-year period is the homogeneity of Conrad's vision, even when the fiction is of uneven quality. . . . None of this would be worth stressing, however, unless Conrad's vision as a whole in this period were not excessively subjective, narcissistic, deeply dependent on memory" (451–52). But a constant psychological state does not account for the "uneven quality" of Conrad's work. Although Karl recognizes that factors in addition to introspection were operating, he minimizes their importance. Among these were Conrad's assumptions about his potential audience. His ability to place his work persuaded him that his effort was worthwhile. Karl recognizes that publishers' support stimulated Conrad's productivity and characterizes Pawling's sale of the still unfinished manuscript of *The Rescue* as a "sudden boost" when Conrad was working on *Lord Jim* and "Heart of Darkness" (423). Nevertheless, Karl separates rhetorical factors from creation: "What we are suggesting for Conrad in this period is such an intense immersion in the powers of his own imagination that he left behind all conscious intentions, all statements of motivation, all planned theories of art and his position within it" (451). The ideological dichotomy between art and money causes Karl to separate Conrad's art from all rhetorical concerns.

Karl's aesthetic assumptions lead him to connect Marlow exclusively to subjective functions. Karl's interpretation is that Marlow was an alter-ego who provided a surrogate for Conrad's memory and imagination: "Conrad descends narcissistically into his own world by means of Marlow, who in his turn has already descended into a dark, morbid underworld. . . . Whatever is outside, in phenomena, is inside, in imagination and wish fulfillment" (451). Similarly, Zdzislaw Najder mentions Polish yarns as an influence on Conrad's use of Marlow, yet he insists, "For a biographer, however, the psychological aspect is more important: in what way did the advent of Marlow help Conrad to overcome his crisis?" (230). Since this type of biographical approach seeks the genesis of the text in the author's private experience, it fails to account for its reception.

Reviewing the critical response to Marlow, Ian Watt balances Marlow's psychological function and his rhetorical effect: "But Marlow is much more than a device for circumventing the modern taboo on authorial moralising; he is also a means of allowing his author to express himself more completely than ever before; through Marlow Conrad discovered a new kind of relation to his audience, and one which enabled him to be more fully himself" (212). Watt links the psychological impulse to self-expression with the rhetorical aim of producing a specific effect on a particular audience: "The first Marlow story, 'Youth,' was also the first story which Conrad ever wrote with a particular group of readers—that of *Blackwood's*—in mind. This defined audience may have given Conrad the initial psychological impetus towards dramatising a fictional situation in which a narrator rather like Conrad addresses an audience rather like that of *Blackwood's"* (212).

What Conrad gained from Marlow is clear if we compare his embedded narratives to the omniscient point of view in his earliest work. *Almayer's Folly,* published in 1895, suffers from narrative inconsistencies. To emphasize character rather than action, Conrad reports events as they are remembered. Yet lacking a center of consciousness, the narrative shifts viewpoints at random:

> His anger was dead within him, and he felt ashamed of his outburst, yet relieved to think that now he had laid clear before his daughter the inner meaning of his life. He thought so in perfect good faith, deceived by the emotional estimate of his motives, unable to see the crookedness of his ways, the unreality of his aims, the futility of his regrets. (102)

The shift from Almayer's feelings to the narrator's judgments violates the reader's expectations. The next passage repeats the inconsistency; at the semicolon the point of view switches from Almayer to the narrator:

> And now his heart was filled only with a great tenderness and love for his daughter. He wanted to see her miserable, and to share with her his despair; but he wanted it only as all weak natures long for a companionship in misfortune with beings innocent of its cause. (102)

Similarly, in the 1897 "An Outpost of Progress" the narrator awkwardly observes of a Sierra Leone native: "Makola, taciturn and impenetrable, despised the two white men," and he "cherished in his innermost heart the worship of evil spirits" (214). While it would be possible for a narrator to infer hatred from even a taciturn and impenetrable man, it would be impossible to know what he worshiped in his innermost heart; only an omniscient narrator could know this, but the text denies omniscience: "They believed their words. Everybody shows a respectful deference to certain sounds that he and his fellows can make. But about feelings people really know nothing" (226).

Marlow allowed Conrad to regulate the relationship between narrator and reader. In addition to the character's symbolic and psychological significance, the use of Marlow as an embedded narrator served a rhetorical purpose for Conrad. Just as Conrad found that he had to conceive of his audience narrowly, so Marlow specifies his audience in the text. Marlow both illustrates and solves Conrad's rhetorical dilemma. In the works he narrates, Marlow adopts a tone suitable for a specific audience. Addressing professional men who have had some experience at sea, Marlow assumes a bond with a class that crosses national boundaries. Marlow's refrain in *Lord Jim* that Jim is "one of us" establishes an artificial community of values and experiences to fill a void.[5] Like Conrad, Marlow is a storyteller who has to define his audience before he can address it in terms he thinks it will understand. In fact, Conrad's actual readership has always been far broader than his narrators stipulate, but by imagining particular narrators and readers, he was able to make rhetorical decisions.

In this period, Conrad continued to stress the need to navigate between the writer's idea and the reader's understanding: "Every truth requires some pretence to make it live" (*Letters* 2:352). His initial intention to write accurately about what he knew intimately was insufficient; he had to alter his perceptions, even distort them, to make them seem true to the reader: "And conviction is found (for others—not for the author) only in certain contradictions and irrelevancies to the general conception of character (or characters) and of the subject" (*Letters* 2:359).

The difficulty of distinguishing economic and aesthetic motives is also apparent in Conrad's letters to Blackwood. When writing both *Lord Jim* and *Nostromo,* Conrad explained his aesthetic intentions in relation to their effect on the reader. For example, he told Blackwood that he shaped the ending of *Lord Jim* with the reader in mind: "It is my opinion that in the working out of the catastrophe psychologic disquisition should have no place. The reader ought to know enough by that time" (*Letters* 2:283). Comparing *Lord Jim* to "Youth" and "Heart of Darkness," Conrad again linked his rhetorical and aesthetic intentions:

> The structure of it is a little loose—this however need not detract from its interest—from the "general reader" point of view. The question of *art* is so endless, so involved and so obscure that one is tempted to turn one's face resolutely away from it. I've certainly an idea—apart

from the idea and the subject of the story—which guides me in my writing, but I would be hard put to it if requested to give it out in the shape of a fixed formula. After all in this as in every other human endeavour one is answerable only to one's conscience. (*Letters* 2:193–94)

Pulled in two directions, Conrad asserted his interest in the "general reader" but undermined this assertion by putting the words in quotes and insisting he wrote for his own conscience anyway.

David Meldrum, Blackwood's editor, believed Conrad would be worth supporting. The author had received £250 for serial rights and expected another £100 for book publication of *The Rescue* (*Letters* 2:54). Meldrum reported on *Lord Jim,* "commercially speaking, it is good, I think" (Blackburn 107). Sales justified his opinion. The first edition of 2,100 copies sold out, and two months later a second impression of 1,050 copies was ordered (Blackburn 116). Meldrum assured Blackwood that "Conrad is a man whose coming into his own may take very long but is bound to result one day" (Blackburn 116). A few weeks later he elaborated his opinion: "I wish I could believe that he would ever be 'popular' in the popular sense, but he is too good for that. On the other hand, it would seem that over 'Lord Jim' he is coming into his own quicker than so 'unfashionable' and clever an author [has] any right to expect in these days" (Blackburn 122). Meldrum's explanations indicate that Conrad was successful with a discriminating minority audience, smaller than a popular audience but larger than a coterie.

Conrad told Meldrum that he dared not expect commercial success from *Jim*: "One decent success with a book would give me a chance to breathe freely. But will it ever come? I fear that from this vol: I must not expect relief" (*Letters* 2:254). Suggesting one reason that many authors portray publishers as adversaries, Conrad tactfully absolved Blackwood's of blame:

> If Jim has any selling success (which I doubt) I would have a clear road to run after the end of the *Rescue*. Otherwise I can see I shall have a difficult existence before me. Sometimes I feel utterly crushed at the prospect; and yet I can not but feel that I've been exceptionally fortunate in the appreciation my work has met with, and in the friendliness and generosity of my publishers. Surely if I go under I shan't

have the divine consolation of railing bitterly at the unkindness of mankind. This, as you perceive, is a serious disadvantage. (*Letters* 2:289)

Flattering his publisher, Conrad assumed responsibility for his successes as well as his failures.

Lord Jim received the kind of critical acclaim Conrad was beginning to expect. The novel's appeal to a discriminating audience was not the least of its attractions. *The Manchester Guardian* notice began:

> Mr. Joseph Conrad's work has long been known to novel readers who search for their literature, and to them the publication of *Lord Jim* may rank as a memorable event. It is not to be accepted easily, it cannot be read in a half dose, and by the great public which multiplies editions it may remain neglected or unknown. Yet it is of such remarkable originality and merit that one may look for an emphasis of critical opinion which, as in the case of Mr. Meredith, can force a great reputation in the face of popular apathy or distaste. (Karl 509)

The reviewer pays tribute to serious fiction's ability to command a durable audience, if not a popular one. This achievement had economic value too. Such praise was enough to convince Blackwood to continue to lend Conrad money.

As critical esteem sustained Conrad's career, he learned to use this reputation to increase his price. He wrote Blackwood: "I am read for my quality and cannot regard anything else. My quality is my truth. The rest may go" (*Letters* 2:413). Conrad stressed his ability to maintain the quality of his art as if it were a product; he was trying to sound businesslike to win the confidence of a businessman. Buttressing financial arguments with aesthetic justification, Conrad sought larger advances.

When pressed to deliver his manuscript, however, Conrad articulated the burden placed on him by the example of Victorian novelists. To escape it, he defended his length and complexity by comparing himself to great Victorians, yet he pleaded for time by calling himself a modern:

> I am long in my development. What of that? Is not Thackeray's penny worth of mediocre fact drowned in an ocean of twaddle? And yet he lives. And Sir Walter, himself, was not the writer of concise

anecdotes I fancy. And G. Elliot [*sic*]—is she as swift as the present public (incapable of fixing its attention for five consecutive minutes) requires us to be at the cost of all honesty, of all truth, and even the most elementary conception of art? But these are great names. I don't compare myself with them. I am *modern,* and I would rather recall Wagner the musician and Rodin the Sculptor who both had to starve a little in their day—and Whistler the painter who made Ruskin the critic foam at the mouth with scorn and indignation. They too have arrived. They had to suffer for being "new." (*Letters* 2:418)

Driven to contradiction, Conrad demanded as much time as the Victorians had, yet he aligned himself with the moderns. He admitted that contemporary readers lacked the Victorians' patience, yet he invoked the Romantic model of the artist as martyr whose poverty and suffering were the penalty for being original. He also declared that as a professional author he was confident the quality of his work would ultimately win an audience large enough to justify the publisher's concessions.

His assertions proved true. Six months later Meldrum confirmed them in a letter to Blackwood:

I am especially glad about "Youth". But I knew Conrad was good—in fact "Youth" I hold to be the most notable book we have published since George Eliot, and so do other judges. "Lord Jim" and "Youth" will go on selling for twenty years, I have no doubt; and it will become a question soon whether they ought not to be put in more popular—say 3/6d—form, like "Ships". That appears to be the recognised method with the works of men of his high, tho' not popular, repute. (Blackburn 172–73)

If not bestsellers, his novels could justify themselves commercially as steady sellers.

Critical acclaim did not end Conrad's difficulties with publishers. More confident, he demanded more money and more time. In contrast to Victorian writers who earned literary independence through sales, Conrad, like Joyce and Lawrence, had more acrimonious relationships with publishers after receiving critical recognition. Karl attributes some of the blame for publishing disputes to Conrad: his "difficulty was not in the sums he obtained as advances and for serial rights but in the slowness of his production, usually no more than

1,500 to 2,000 words a week" (423). Conrad also blamed his predicament on his pace: the problem was "my inability to work fast enough to get my living. It is ridiculous and sad and wearisome, and that it is true does not make it any less offensive" (*Letters* 2:173). Although Conrad wrote rapidly enough to produce a book a year, more than most popular writers, he wanted more money than this pace could generate. Karl justly observes, "The money that came in was certainly not commensurate with Conrad's worth as an artist, but on the other hand, it could have been sufficient with more careful attention to outlay" (547). In short, his work appealed to a large enough public to support him. He reached a viable public, if not a mass audience, and publishers were willing to subsidize him.

Blackwood accepted Conrad's excuses for delays but explicitly contrasted him with his Victorian predecessors: "I have always looked upon the writing of fiction as something not to be bounded altogether by time or space notwithstanding my old friend Anthony Trollope who went to a desk as a shoemaker goes to his last" (Blackburn 29). Writing in 1898, Blackwood remembered Trollope and his type clearly. Like Garnett, he paid tribute to the vagaries of the artist while reminding Conrad of the duties of the professional. Although younger than Blackwood, Conrad also measured himself against Victorian standards of workmanship. In 1905 he compared himself to Trollope:

> That I cannot work with the regularity and certitude of an Anthony Trollope is a defect purely temperamental; but that I desire to avoid the most remote appearance of being the XXth century edition of Johnson's Mr Savage you cannot but understand and approve (even if you find my dread exaggerated) knowing as you do the irresponsible judgments passed every day upon the living and the dead alike. (*Letters* 3:261)

Conrad wanted the income of popular novelists to buy time to write the kind of complex work that appealed to a minority audience. As Lewes's Principle of Sincerity predicts, when Conrad deliberately attempted to write just for the marketplace, he failed. Trying to copy Guy Bothby's formula, he confessed failure: "I can't get the secret of this fellow's manner. It's beyond me, how he does it!"

(Garnett 25). He could not imitate the qualities he knew popular novels needed—easy style, plenty of action, romantic atmosphere, a happy ending (Karl 525). As eager as he was for popular success, Conrad could not produce the kind of novels the public seemed to prefer.

Unable to control his business affairs, Conrad became associated with J. B. Pinker in 1899. Pinker went further than most agents, taking charge of Conrad's finances to free him to write. To support him until there was a completed manuscript to sell, Pinker paid him per thousand words submitted each week. Karl's estimate of Pinker is hard-headed: "Pinker was an agent, however, not a literary man, and he was more impressed by copy turned in on time (such as Arnold Bennett's) than by grand names. If he supported Conrad in the face of his better financial instincts, it was because he believed, finally, in Conrad and not because he thought he was supporting great literature" (582). But in view of the financial burden Conrad imposed, only literary judgment could have convinced Pinker that Conrad would eventually repay him. To believe in Conrad was to believe in his work. Blending his own judgments with Conrad's, Karl writes, "Pinker provided a modicum of control, a businessman, a Jew who would make sure profit outbalanced loss" (489). The gratuitous religious identification belongs to a cluster of stereotypes accompanying the polarity of art and money.

Like Joyce and Lawrence, Conrad sought Pinker's help yet resented him for giving it. Conrad hated being dependent on Pinker, and at times he hated Pinker for permitting him to depend on him. He responded to Pinker's questions about delays with outraged dignity:

> If you don't want the bother of my stuff saddled with my other imperfections tell me to go to the devil. That won't offend me and I'll go as soon as ever you had your money back. But don't address me as if I were a man lost in sloth, ignorance or folly. Were you as rich as Croesus and as omnipotent as all the editors rolled into one I would not let such a tone pass without resenting it in the most outspoken manner. And don't write to me of failure, confound it! because you and I have very different notions of failure. (*Letters* 2:370–71)

Artistic identity sustained his hauteur; the artist was superior to others no matter how much money he owed them. Conrad continually told Pinker he was close to finishing his current project. Surely Pinker did not expect him to deliver copy as promised—none of Conrad's friends believed his optimistic estimates, and Pinker was more experienced than they were.

Despite publishers' continuous support, Conrad lost control of his work by living on advances. When publishers granted his requests for money, Conrad felt pressure as well as gratitude. Loans burdened him with the obligation to produce copy too quickly. Making promises he could not keep, he felt dishonorable, but mounting debts and expenses made him continue the practice. Working under financial pressure, Conrad considered his later work inferior. The need to sell what he had written before he was satisfied with it made him feel he was succumbing to the "Grub Street aspect" of publishing.[6]

Relinquishing control of his work and permitting Pinker to sell everything as he thought best, Conrad gained the measure of freedom from financial worry he needed to write his longer works. He continued to promise Pinker salable work but still could not control its length or complexity. At the same time he assured Pinker he would meet completion dates with commercial novels, in letters to his friends he expressed doubts about finishing or selling current work. His characteristic pattern was to develop an idea for a short story, assuring Pinker he would soon have something to sell. Inevitably, the idea would seize him, complicate itself, and require thousands of words to work itself out. However differently they are judged today, *The Secret Agent* and *Under Western Eyes* were written the same way as *Lord Jim*, and *Victory* grew from a story called "Dollars" that Conrad started when he was reviewing galleys for *Chance* in 1913. As he said in 1907, "I am long because my thought is always multiple . . ." (*Letters* 3:492). Despite the pressure of debt, Conrad could not stop elaborating. Finishing quickly was in his financial interest, yet length was also an asset because novels brought in more money than stories.

Frustrated that no correlation between talent and income existed, he periodically expressed despair that he would ever realize his aesthetic and rhetorical intentions. Of his forthcoming volumes of stories, one for Blackwood, one for Heinemann, he said in 1902: "I don't believe either in their popularity or in their merit" (*Letters* 2:424). Seeking refuge in the privacy of the writer, he wrote that "one writes for oneself even when one writes to live and in the hope of being read by an immortal multitude"; the author's "solitary thought cannot be imparted to a public" (*Letters* 3:13). Yet he chided H. G. Wells (of all people) for deliberately limiting his public:

> Why should you say that you write only for people who think this or that: Who feel this or the other thing? And if you even think so—and so intend—there is no necessity to *say* so. That's what I mean by saying that such a declaration serves your sincerity at the expense of the truth—which is in you to expound and propagate. After all why should you preach to people already convinced? That sort of thing leads only to a sort of high priesthood in a clique and it should be left to people who seek simply the satisfaction of their vanity. It is just to the unbelievers that *you* should preach; and believe me that no one is too benighted (emotionally or rationally) to be spoken to with some effect by him who *can* speak. (*Letters* 3:63)

Lower expectations of readers did not necessarily produce more accessible texts, but they did alter Conrad's conception of himself. Losing respect for his reader, he also lost respect for his work. His statements of intention became more contradictory. He asserted his integrity yet confessed to mercenary schemes. Constant pressure to supply copy to redeem his advances made him feel that he rushed his work to press. Depressed and unsure of himself, he wrote Garnett in 1902: "My expression has become utterly worthless: it is time for the money to come rolling in" (*Letters* 2:424). The book he was writing at the time, however, was *Nostromo*. Apologizing for the faults of *Under Western Eyes,* he told John Galsworthy: "But good work takes time. . . . This I could not afford to do. I went on the obvious lines and on these lines I developed my narrative to give it some sort of verisimilitude. In other words I offered to sell my soul for half a crown—and now I have neither the soul nor the coin—for the novel is not finished yet. A fool's bargain . . ." (*Letters* 4:155). Later Conrad blamed his dissatisfaction with the progress of *Victory* on his need for money; he told Bertrand Russell: "seduced by that tempter's gold, I allowed myself to be drawn into 'fixing' a date for delivery of an unfinished novel—for the first time in my life" (*Letters* 5:345). Although it was hardly the first time, Conrad used the dichotomy of art and money to excuse work he feared would fail. He assumed others would understand that he had to compromise the quality of his work if he were writing for money.

The more Conrad doubted his readers' ability to understand him, the more he tried to anticipate and control their reactions. Describing the writer's relationship to society in 1905, he insisted on the writer's obligation to readers. As Conrad learned more about the public, he tried to make his fiction familiar to their experience: "This world cannot be made otherwise than in his own image: it is fated to remain individual and a little mysterious, and yet it must resemble something already familiar to the experience, the thoughts and the sensations of his readers" (Karl 586–87). His rationale appears in advice to another writer as he argues that his suggestions are justified by the public's needs:

> You may not like a full close—but the ordinary reader expects it. And the ordinary reader also wants the nail hit on the head before his very eyes simply in order that he should *see* the nail. Later on you will realize the inconceivable stupidity of the common reader—the man who forks out the half-crown. (*Letters* 4:52)

Correcting his earlier assumption that with skill he could make readers see what he saw, however complex his vision, he found that to reach a wide audience he had to demand less of it. This strategy was not simply a concession to increase sales; it also reflected his continuing effort to establish a bond with his audience. Throughout his career Conrad believed what he told Garnett in 1911: "control of the public's (audience, readers) attention is in a sense the beginning and end of artistic method" (*Letters* 4:422).

The changes in Marlow from *Lord Jim* (1900) to *Chance* (1913) indicate the stages in Conrad's estimate of his readers. As Marlow reiterates in *Lord Jim,* Jim is "one of us." In contrast to his tacit assumption of a community here, in *Chance* Marlow himself must be explained by Powell, another narrator. Powell describes Marlow for the reader:

> In the full light of the room I saw in his eyes that slightly mocking expression with which he habitually covers up his sympathetic

impulses of mirth and pity before the unreasonable complications the idealism of mankind puts into the simple but poignant problem of conduct on this earth. (325)

In the thirteen years between these novels, Conrad's expectations of the reader fell. Aiming for a wider audience than his earlier work had reached, he tried to adopt popular strategies. Although he felt his deliberate efforts to make the novel popular diminished its aesthetic value, reviewers praised its attention to form and narrative technique. It was judged one of his most modern, and C. E. Montague wrote that in *Chance* Conrad carried his narrative technique "further than ever" (Karl 743). Conrad believed he had copied popular models, but reviewers discerned aesthetic complexity.

Suffering great ambivalence while writing *Chance*, Conrad was contradictory in his letters. Although he disparaged the book after it was published, writing one friend, "I am glad you find Chance tolerable. I don't" (*Letters* 5:336), he alternated these defensive comments with promises that it would be salable, if not popular:

> *Chance* itself will be altogether different in tone and treatment [from *The Secret Agent*] of course, but it will be saleable I believe. By the end of September you will have a really considerable lot of it to show. Of course it will not be on popular lines. Nothing of mine can be, I fear. But even Meredith ended by getting his sales. Now, I haven't Meredith's delicacy and that's a point in my favour. I reckon I may make certain of the support of the Press for the next few years. The young men who are coming in to write criticisms are in my favour so far. At least all of whom I've heard are. I don't get in the way of established reputations. . . . There is nothing in me but a turn of mind which whether valuable or worthless can not be imitated. (*Letters* 3:460)

Aiming for solidarity with a wider audience than his earlier work had reached, he adopted popular strategies. He tried to choose an appealing title, subject, and ending. Instead of another sea yarn, he decided to write about a young girl. He admitted changing the ending to make it "nicer": "I am thinking of the public" (*Letters* 5:49). Garnett believed that despite eulogistic notices, probably the "figure of the lady on the 'jacket' of *Chance* (1914) did more to bring the novel into popular favor than the long review by Sir Sidney Colvin in *The Observer*" (Garnett 15).

Chance rewarded Conrad's publisher and agent for their confidence in him. The English edition sold thirteen thousand copies in two years. Karl discounts this fourfold increase in Conrad's usual sales figures as falling short of "best-sellerdom" (740), but Conrad took pride in the figures: "Seven editions of *Chance*=12000 copies (to date)—which for England is very good and for me something absolutely fabulous" (*Letters* 5:351). *Chance* won immediate critical acclaim as well as high sales, yet Conrad wrote Galsworthy:

> How I would have felt about it ten or eight years ago I can't say. Now I can't even pretend I am elated. If I had Nostromo, The Nigger or Lord Jim in my desk or only in my head I would feel differently no doubt. As to the commercial side: Methuen made a ridiculous advertising splash (which was jeered at in the provincial press) and in the sixth week stopped advertising. They confess to 12,500 copies printed . . . but how much of that is sold I don't know. (*Letters* 5:365)

He bitterly regretted that the benefits of reputation were not retroactive. Judging his earlier books superior, he felt cheated of his proper remuneration, which would have made both his domestic and artistic life easier.

As an artist claiming his due from society, he used his aesthetic reputation to raise his price. Negotiating the price for serializing *Chance,* Conrad told the new editor of *The English Review* that in 1899 "B'wood's maga: accepted my *Lord Jim* a much closer knit and more complicated work with a remote psychology—sailors, Malays, and so on—whereas *Chance* is English in personages and locality, much easier to follow and understand. It was a very new form then; and yet old Maga had the audacity to take it up when we all were much less 'advanced' than we are now and Conrad was a practically unknow[n] writer" (*Letters* 5:45). The superior tone, the guarantee of propriety, and the confidence in the value of his work were all elements of his attitude to his audience. Here Conrad separated each book and attempted to put a price on it according to its merits, but other letters indicate he knew his works acquired a cumulative value greater than any single work possessed. The reason he was able to earn so much for his later work was that his earlier work was so highly acclaimed.

As he aimed at a wider audience more cynically, he invoked the myth of the artist's indifference to the public more tendentiously. Such romanticized pronouncements became more frequent as he tailored his work to suit average readers. In contrast to his initial unwillingness to live in a garret, he glorified suffering now that he was out of danger:

> Suffering is an attribute almost a condition of greatness, of devotion, of an altogether self-forgetful sacrifice to that remorseless fidelity to the truth of his own sensations at whatever [*sic*] cost of pain or contumely which for me is the whole credo of the artist. (*Letters* 5:239)

In contrast to his frank concern with money while struggling with *Nigger of the "Narcissus," Lord Jim,* and *Nostromo,* in 1907 while working on *Chance* and consciously writing for a wide audience, Conrad claimed he was not thinking of money: "While I am writing I am not thinking of money. I couldn't if I would. The thing once written I admit that I want to see it bring in as much money as possible and to have as much *effect* as possible" (*Letters* 3:481). Determined to resist the antithesis between popularity and quality, he insisted that his desire for sales did not require any compromise of artistic integrity. Earlier, he could acknowledge his concern with money because he did not feel that it influenced his work.

The 1920 preface to *Chance* reaffirmed Conrad's rhetorical intentions, despite his increased awareness of the difficulty of achieving them. Echoing his preface to *Nigger of the "Narcissus,"* he demonstrated the constancy of his desire to communicate with his readers. By 1920, however, popular success made him defensive about this strong rhetorical aim. He correctly anticipated that popularity would make readers think he had compromised his aesthetic standards for sales. The introduction to *Chance* expresses his unswerving commitment to a constant rhetorical goal, but he adds a more vehement defense of solidarity against the ideology of the artist as martyr: "what I always feared most was drifting unconsciously into the position of a writer for a limited coterie; a position which would have been odious to me as throwing a doubt on the soundness of my belief in the solidarity of all mankind in simple ideas and in sincere emotions" (x–xi). Unwilling to accept the limited audience that initially appreciated what he heard, felt, and saw, in the 1920 preface he reaffirmed his belief in the solidarity of all mankind and implicitly defended the need to make his work more accessible to reach a wide public.

Learning more about the public with each book, he gradually found that solidarity was harder to achieve than he had initially assumed. Conrad inveighed against the public, but he could not renounce it. He wrote John Galsworthy in 1910:

> A public is not to be found in a class, caste, clique or type. The public is (or are?) individuals. *Le public introuvable* is only *introuvable* simply because it is all humanity. And no artist can give it what it wants because humanity doesn't know what it wants. But it will swallow anything. It will swallow Hall Caine and John Galsworthy, Victor Hugo and Martin Tupper. It is an ostrich, a clown, a giant, a bottomless sack. It is sublime. It has apparently no eyes and no entrails, like a slug, and yet it can weep and suffer. It has swallowed Christianity, Buddhism, Mahomedanism, and the Gospel of Mrs Eddy. And it is perfectly capable from the height of its secular stability to look down upon the artist as a mere windlestraw! (*Letters* 4:385)

The indifference of the marketplace was far more annoying than its preferences. It would buy anything. To reach a wide public, he tried to simplify his work, yet this strategy did not necessarily produce simpler novels. Like other modernists, Conrad vilified the kind of writing that was merely popular but never disdained popularity itself.

CHAPTER THREE

James Joyce:
Fame and Notoriety

Most accounts of Joyce's career betray the bias of hindsight. They accept the dichotomy between art and money Joyce expressed at A. S. W. Rosenbach's expense in this rhyme:

> Rosy Brook he bought a book
> Though he didn't know how to spell it.
> Such is the lure of literature
> To the lad who can buy it and sell it.[1]

Although the exhumation of details about an author's personal life—what Foucault calls the "author-function" (148)—cannot alter his oeuvre, Joyce's life has been used to sustain myths about his writing. The halo of genius blinds his admirers to traits all too evident to his contemporaries. In the morality play Joyce made of his life, he cast all who failed to hail his genius as villains. If the record is not read retrospectively, however, Joyce appears as an unknown but highly recommended young writer whose career progressed steadily until he faced censorship. The purpose of reexamining Joyce's publishing troubles from the publishers' point of view is not to argue that he should have conformed to their demands—his work has entered the modernist canon *because* it defied them. But by analyzing Joyce's career as an example of the modernist author's dilemma, we can

begin to question the myth of martyrdom that has become the litmus test for the serious artist.

Joyce embarked on his career as his predecessors had: he cultivated the influence of established authors and editors. Enlisting
George Russell, W. B. Yeats, Lady Gregory, and George Moore,
Joyce tried to exploit the Irish literary revival to promote his reputation. In Richard Ellmann's judgment, "The members of the Irish
literary movement were doing their best for Joyce, but all were to
discover that he was not a man to be helped with impunity" (104).
Russell expressed their characteristic forbearance: "I expect to see my
young genius on Monday and will find out more about him. I
wouldn't be his Messiah for a thousand million pounds. He would
be always criticising the bad taste of his deity" (Ellmann 99–100).

Although Joyce's attitude discouraged assistance, many who were
part of the literary establishment tolerated his pride because they, too,
considered it part of the artist's persona. Introducing Joyce to Yeats
in 1902, Russell assumed Yeats would also accept Joyce's behavior:
"I think you would find this youth of twenty-one with his assurance
and self-confidence rather interesting" (Ellmann 100). Yeats, however, was less dazzled than Russell and remarked, "Such a colossal
self-conceit with such a Lilliputian literary genius I never saw com-
bined in one person" (Ellmann 101). Despite his initial reaction,
Yeats soon befriended Joyce. Long before he had published anything
to justify it, Joyce began to enjoy the benefits of his reputation as a
genius.

The most material benefit was a commission from Russell, who
had read and admired parts of "Stephen Hero." Russell requested
something simple for the *Irish Homestead* that would not shock his
readers. Obsequious before the novice author, Russell wrote: "It is
easily earned money if you can write fluently and don't mind play-
ing to the common understanding and liking for once in a way. You
can sign it any name you like as a pseudonym" (Ellmann 163).
Adhering to the creed that genius was above the common reader,
Russell apologized for requesting something suited to his market.[2]

Joyce, however, wanted both the money and the readers Russell
offered, so he accepted the assignment. He explicitly stated his
rhetorical intention: "I call the series *Dubliners* to betray the soul of

that hemiplegia or paralysis which many consider a city" (*Selected Letters* 22). Writing the stories with specific Dubliners in mind, Joyce was so successful in betraying the soul of his birthplace that readers complained, and Russell had to cancel the series after the first three stories appeared.

Defying social and literary conventions was both an act of individualism and an act of aggression but not a sign of indifference. Joyce often insisted that his commitment to living out his moral values was purely an affirmation of individualism, but it was also a form of vengeance: "Give me for Christ' sake a pen and an ink-bottle and some peace of mind and then, by the crucified Jaysus, if I don't sharpen that little pen and dip it into fermented ink and write tiny little sentences about the people who betrayed me send me to hell" (*Selected Letters* 76). In another letter he revealed both his desire for revenge and his attempt to conceal this motive in exalted terms: "The Dublin papers will object to my stories as to a caricature of Dublin life. Do you think there is any truth in this? At times the spirit directing my pen seems to me so plainly mischievous that I am almost prepared to let the Dublin critics have their way" (*Selected Letters* 70). His ambivalence emerges in the space of a few sentences. On one hand, he sees the "mischievous" streak in his stories; on the other, he defends it as an expression of his inner nature rather than as a reaction against society: "The struggle against conventions in which I am at present involved was not entered into by me so much as a protest against those conventions as with the intention of living in conformity with my moral nature" (*Selected Letters* 70). Even Harriet Weaver, his staunchest patron, suspected that he needed to think of himself as a martyr to write, that he had a weakness "for courting betrayal" (Lidderdale 306).

Committing his life to a literary career, Joyce did not intend to write for a coterie. His earliest rhetorical position resembled Flaubert's model of the artist as professional who instructed the public. Joyce singled out Ibsen for his "absolute indifference to public canons of art, friends and shibboleths" (*Selected Letters* 7). Just as Ibsen was indifferent to public opinion but committed to exposing his society's hypocrisy, Joyce also intended to address the general public because his goal was to recreate Irish character: "I am one of the writers of this generation who are perhaps creating at last a conscience in the soul of this wretched race" (*Selected Letters* 204). In *A Portrait of the Artist as a Young Man,* Joyce allows Stephen Dedalus to echo this aim in a diary entry: "I go to encounter for the millionth time the reality of experience and to forge in the smithy of my soul the uncreated conscience of my race" (253). At the same time, Cranley's remark about Stephen also describes Joyce: "To discover the mode of life or of art whereby your spirit could express itself in unfettered freedom" (246). Thus, Stephen embodies the contradictory claims of social responsibility and self-expression. While sales were necessary to produce a social impact, the unfettered freedom of writing for oneself became the litmus test of the true artist.

Joyce believed that Thomas Hardy managed to combine this ideal of the artist with the vocation of the novelist:

> But whatever diversity of judgment may exist about his work (if any does exist), it is none the less evident to all that Hardy demonstrated in his attitude of the poet in relation to his public, an honourable example of integrity and self-esteem of which we other clerks are always a little in need, especially in a period when the reader seems to content himself with less and less of the poor written word and when, in consequence, the writer tends to concern himself more and more with the great questions which, for all that, adjust themselves very well without his aid. (*Selected Letters* 329n)

Joyce's contempt for the rhetoric of domesticity, patriotism, and religion—a trinity he despised—did not initially include indifference to the rhetorical effect of his writing on readers. He wanted to be independent of his audience to change it. His self-proclaimed exile was a strategy for staging an assault on Ireland. Since his initial purpose was social criticism, publication was essential to his objective.

When Joyce submitted *Dubliners* to Grant Richards in 1905, he fully expected an uproar, but it was to be a public uproar. He claimed that his subject was important, original, profitable, and offensive:

> I do not think that any writer has yet presented Dublin to the world. It has been a capital of Europe for thousands of years, it is supposed to be the second city of the British Empire and it is nearly three times as big as Venice. Moreover, on account of many circumstances which I cannot detail here, the expression "Dubliner" seems to me to have

some meaning and I doubt whether the same can be said for such words as "Londoner" and "Parisian" both of which have been used by writers as titles. From time to time I see in publishers' lists announcements of books on Irish subjects, so that I think people might be willing to pay for the special odour of corruption which, I hope, floats over my stories. (*Selected Letters* 78–79)

The first part of this passage might have been written by an alderman, but Joyce punctures the brag about Dublin as a world capital with a barbed accusation.

Grant Richards received a favorable reader's report that resembled Joyce's description, except the reader's recommendation found nothing controversial in the stories: "Dublin has been a neglected capital but the author portrays it in these stories with sympathy and patience which equal his knowledge of Dublin, its idiom, its people, its streets, and its little houses. . . . The purpose of these stories is not combative, and, as artistic sincerity has been placed above other cries in the street, they are written with truthfulness that cannot be gainsaid" ("Dubliners"). Failing to detect the bitterness Joyce intended and readers of the *Irish Homestead* discerned, the editor gave Richards no warning of trouble ahead. Richards did not object to the stories until his printer refused to set the type.

The objections Richards eventually conveyed to Joyce were legal, not artistic. In the ensuing negotiations for revisions to make the book conform to standards of decency, Joyce restated the high-minded side of his purpose:

My intention was to write a chapter of the moral history of my country and I chose Dublin for the scene because that city seemed to me the centre of paralysis. . . . I have written it for the most part in a style of scrupulous meanness and with the conviction that he is a very bold man who dares to alter in the presentment, still more to deform, whatever he has seen and heard. (*Selected Letters* 83)

Limiting his "mischievous" motives to "a style of scrupulous meanness," he claimed that the objectionable passages were simply reflections of reality, not his inventions. If there were offensive scenes, Dublin was to blame, not the author. Despite this disclaimer, he continued, "I have come to the conclusion that I cannot write without offending people" (*Selected Letters* 83).

Offending people was an inextricable part of Joyce's rhetorical purpose. In response to Richards's request that he delete "bloody," he argued that he had used it to create a specific effect on the reader: "The word, the exact expression I have used, is in my opinion the one expression in the English language which can create on the reader the effect which I wish to create" (*Selected Letters* 85). Facing a crusader for freedom of expression, Richards focused on the use of "bloody" in "Grace." Instead of simply eliminating the word to expedite publication, Joyce defended it, pointing out that it also appeared in "Ivy Day in the Committee Room" and "Two Gallants." He may have hoped the parallel cases would persuade Richards to allow the word, but of course, Richards extended his objections to these stories as well. Both men refused to yield. Richards expressed his impatience in practical terms: "If I had written your stories I should certainly wish to be able to afford your attitude" (*Selected Letters* 84n). Joyce framed his rejoinder in artistic terms: "I have written my book with considerable care, in spite of a hundred difficulties and in accordance with what I understand to be the classical tradition of my art" (*Letters of J.J.* 1:60). As a result, Richards has been cast as the philistine, but Joyce was at least an agent-provocateur.

Grant Richards declined *Dubliners* on September 24, 1906, with regrets and hopes for a novel rather than stories, but he declined it nonetheless. Joyce sought legal recourse but was informed he had a weak case. He also turned to Arthur Symons for practical advice. Symons—hardly a philistine—suggested that Joyce try to meet Richards's objections as much as he could "without vitally damaging your work" (*Selected Letters* 115).

By defining his literary conscience in opposition to his publishing interests, Joyce made cooperation with an editor impossible. The financial rewards of cooperation introduced the metaphor of prostitution, commonly used by writers who were uneasy selling creative work: "Of course I would gladly see the book in print and of course I would like to make money by it. But, on the other hand, I have very little intention of prostituting whatever talent I may have to the public" (*Selected Letters* 86). With the publisher explaining legal issues and Joyce professing his sincerity, an impasse was inevitable. The conflict between ideologies of the expressive artist and the professional author persisted in this kind of exchange.

Joyce continued to claim that his rhetorical goal was the moral improvement of his readers, but he linked this goal to aesthetic integrity:

> The points on which I have not yielded are the points which rivet the book together. If I eliminate them what becomes of the chapter of the moral history of my country? I fight to retain them because I believe that in composing my chapter of moral history in exactly the way I have composed it I have taken the first step towards the spiritual liberation of my country. (*Selected Letters* 88)

Accusing Richards of cowardice, Joyce cited a literary antecedent to legitimize his social criticism: "You must allow me to say that I think you are unduly timid. . . . You will not be prosecuted for publishing it. The worst that will happen, I suppose, is that some critic will allude to me as the 'Irish Zola!'" (*Selected Letters* 86). Another letter to Richards stressed his rhetorical goal: "I seriously believe that you will retard the course of civilisation in Ireland by preventing the Irish people from having one good look at themselves in my nicely polished looking-glass" (*Selected Letters* 90). Did these aims absolutely require the word "bloody" in three stories?

Joyce's dilemma was that he had to sell his work, not just to earn a living, but to earn a living as a professional author. He had to publish to prove he was not one more aspiring amateur. Trying to make his contradictory aims compatible, he argued that by flouting conventions he could not only express himself and improve the reader but also increase sales:

> Critics (I think) are fonder of attacking writers than publishers; and, I assure you their attacks on me would in no way hasten my death. Moreover, from the point of view of financial success it seems to me more than probable than [*sic*] an attack, even a fierce and organised attack, on the book by the press would have the effect of interesting the public in it to much better purpose than the tired chorus of imprimaturs with which the critical body greets the appearance of every book which is not dangerous to faith or morals. (*Selected Letters* 88)

Joyce was right on both counts: the book did not provoke an attack, and it would have sold better if it had.

Nevertheless, Joyce saw the justice of some of Richards's objections. Reflecting on Richards's complaint that Dublin was portrayed too bleakly, Joyce conceded the point in a letter to his brother:

> Sometimes thinking of Ireland it seems to me that I have been unnecessarily harsh. I have reproduced (in *Dubliners* at least) none of the attraction of the city for I have never felt at my ease in any city since I left it except in Paris. I have not reproduced its ingenuous insularity and its hospitality. The latter "virtue" so far as I can see does not exist elsewhere in Europe. I have not been just to its beauty: for it is more beautiful naturally in my opinion than what I have seen of England, Switzerland, France, Austria or Italy. And yet I know how useless these reflections are. For were I to rewrite the book as G.R. suggests "in another sense" (where the hell does he get the meaningless phrases he uses) I am sure I should find again what you call the Holy Ghost sitting in the ink-bottle and the perverse devil of my literary conscience sitting on the hump of my pen. (*Selected Letters* 109–10)

He eventually responded to Richards's criticism by writing "The Dead," which portrays the "virtue" of hospitality, however ambiguously. In view of Joyce's reputation, it is ironic that a publisher's suggestion initiated the most widely praised story in *Dubliners*, as an editor's commission had encouraged Joyce to begin the series. Although publishers' objections delayed its publication, *Dubliners* owed its origin and conclusion to editors' suggestions. If these stories had appeared in 1906, even minus "The Dead," which was not written until 1907, he might have followed the usual path to authorship, earning editorial independence by building an audience.

When Richards refused to publish without revisions, Joyce submitted *Dubliners* to other English publishers, who also rejected it. Maunsel and Company, a Dublin firm headed by George Roberts, expressed interest, but Joyce was reluctant to test the manuscript in Ireland. In 1909 he relented and finally signed a contract with Maunsel, but publication was again postponed because the printers balked. Negotiating with Maunsel, Joyce mixed promises and demands. He again defended his use of references to actual people and places as a way to increase the commercial value of the stories. He agreed to "put fictitious names for the few real ones but added that by so doing the selling value in Dublin of the book would go down" (*Selected Letters* 205).

As much as he antagonized publishers, Joyce had an instinct for publicity. He transformed publishers' rejections into his best advertisement. To convince Maunsel to publish, Joyce wrote a letter to two newspapers detailing the acts of censorship he had suffered. Instead of enumerating Richards's demands, he shrewdly chose to address Maunsel's complaint about a disrespectful reference to Edward VII. Hoping to forestall printers' objections, Joyce wrote to the king for permission to publish the passage. The king refused to comment. Joyce then quoted the questioned passage, publishing in newspapers what commercial firms would not print in books. Nevertheless, the stratagem did not reverse Maunsel's decision. Exasperated that every time he agreed to one change Maunsel demanded another, Joyce endured five more years of fruitless negotiation. He wanted publication and sales, but he could not permit himself to seek them directly. They had to be rewards for aesthetic integrity, not ends in themselves.

Publication delays gradually weakened Joyce's rhetorical commitment to his audience. Prevented from selling his work, he had little practical incentive to continue writing. He told Richards, "I assure you, not the least unfortunate effect of this tardy correspondence is that it has brought my own writing into disfavour with myself" (*Selected Letters* 87). Denying the martyrdom he also sought, Joyce vented his frustration: "You cannot imagine I want to continue writing at present. I have written quite enough and before I do any more in that line I must see some reason why—I am not a literary Jesus Christ" (*Selected Letters* 106). Uncertainty about publication discouraged further revision. Joyce wanted to rewrite "After the Race" but feared introducing a new obstacle to publication: "The chase of perfection is very unprofitable" (*Selected Letters* 97). He also wanted to add five pages to "A Painful Case" but explained, "I am not strenuous enough to continue in the face of such continual discouragement" (*Selected Letters* 99). Utterly disheartened, he wrote: "It is impossible for me to write anything in my present circumstances" (*Selected Letters* 121). He needed practical encouragement: "If only my book is published then I will plunge into my novel and finish it"

(*Selected Letters* 204). He was so distraught that he almost destroyed the manuscript of *A Portrait* "in a fit of rage on account of the trouble over *Dubliners*" (*Selected Letters* 247).

Deprived of the validation publication and readers could bestow, Joyce sought other justifications for continuing to write. In the absence of any response except legal objections, he became increasingly independent of external judgment, whether approval or criticism. As the prospect of publication diminished, Joyce more frequently described his purpose as self-expression than as social criticism. Losing his rhetorical motive, he tried to account for his compulsion to write: "Yet I have certain ideas I would like to give form to: not as a doctrine but as the continuation of the expression of myself which I now see I began in *Chamber Music*. These ideas or instincts or intuitions may be purely personal" (*Selected Letters* 151). Whereas Lawrence moved from personal to moral justifications for being sexually explicit, Joyce justified his increasing obscurity in personal terms. Failing to reach his intended audience, he started to attribute his art to an inner source rather than to a public need.

This defense had roots in the Romantic tradition of self-expression. Although Joyce emulated Flaubert's impersonality, he also admired Wordsworth and Shelley (*Selected Letters* 62). In 1905 he had endorsed the Romantic tenet that deep feeling was the essential ingredient of art: "I am sure however that the whole structure of heroism is, and always was, a damned lie and that there cannot be any substitute for the individual passion as the motive power of everything—art and philosophy included" (*Selected Letters* 54). "Temperament" justified his vocation as an artist: "It is possible that the delusion I have with regard to my power to write will be killed by adverse circumstances. But the delusion which will never leave me is that I am an artist by temperament" (*Selected Letters* 77). He realized that the task of writing required material support and painstaking composition as well as deep feeling, but he thought of his calling as something distinct from his actual writing. In the Romantic manner, he asserted that he was an artist by virtue of his inner being, whatever he produced.

In 1913 Richards asked to see *Dubliners* again and finally published it in 1914. Although Richards had procrastinated because he feared prosecution, a worse fate befell the book—poor sales. In 1915 *Dubliners* sold 499 copies, one less than the number at which royalties were due, and fewer were sold the following year. Joyce understandably considered the figures "disastrous," but Richards was "satisfied that the book had 'made a sensation in a small way'" (Ellmann 354). To console Joyce, Richards assured him that few books were selling well because of the war (Ellmann 354n). In fact, the war stimulated the book trade, especially the sale of serious novels and poetry. Despite some good reviews (Magalaner and Kain 55), the public was even less encouraging than publishers had been.

By the time *Dubliners* appeared, Joyce had completed *A Portrait of the Artist*. Between 1905, when he submitted *Dubliners* to Grant Richards, and 1914, when it finally appeared, he recast "Stephen Hero" into *A Portrait* and also drafted parts of *Ulysses*. Recent scholarship indicates that his work on these two books was "more coterminous than we have cared to realize" (Owen 119). Since his first two books were published within a few months of one another, Joyce never had the opportunity to react to readers' responses to *Dubliners* while writing *A Portrait* or the first sections of *Ulysses*.

Despite Joyce's disdain for "mean influences," criticism could have been valuable. For example, Ezra Pound's enthusiastic review of *Dubliners* did not appear in *The Egoist* until *A Portrait* was being serialized there. Finding *Dubliners* consistent with his imagist principles of 1912, Pound admired it primarily for its "clear hard prose" and realism (Read 27–28). He praised Joyce for his "condensation" and "rigorous selection" (Read 29), services Joyce refused to perform in *Ulysses*. Pound articulated a social purpose for modernism when he analyzed the rhetorical effect of realism in *Dubliners* and *A Portrait*: "It is very important that there should be clear, unexaggerated, realistic literature. It is very important that there should be good prose. The hell of contemporary Europe is caused by the lack of representative government in Germany, *and* by the non-existence of decent prose in the German language. Clear thought and sanity depend on clear prose" (Read 90). Joyce, however, had already begun to abandon the very qualities Pound praised in his review.[3]

After *A Portrait* appeared serially in *The Egoist,* H. G. Wells recommended Joyce to his agent, J. B. Pinker. Despite the novel's controversial political and sexual themes, it was recognized as a major work in a familiar tradition, the *Künstlerroman* (Levin, *James Joyce* 41). Pinker and others in commercial publishing recognized its market value immediately, and sales eventually confirmed their judgment. Pinker submitted the manuscript to Duckworth and received a cautious but favorable reply from the reader, Edward Garnett. Explaining his reservations, Garnett wrote that the author "shows us he has art, strength and originality, but this MS. wants time and trouble spent on it, to make it a more finished piece of work, to shape it more carefully as the product of the craftsmanship, mind and imagination of an artist" (Ellmann 404). He encouraged Joyce to revise it and submit it again.

Garnett never expected blind obedience, and his reactions to manuscripts helped many writers improve their final drafts. The critical bias in favor of artistic freedom has faulted Garnett for failing to respect the inviolability of a text which has become canonical, but his criticism was worth considering. Although Garnett anticipated that the public would find the book "a little sordid" and too "unconventional," his substantive suggestions were that it needed "a good deal of pruning" in the earlier portion and a new ending: "there is a complete falling to bits; the pieces of writing and the thoughts are all in pieces and they fall like damp, ineffective rockets" (Ellmann 404). Subsequent criticism has unwittingly corroborated some of these objections. For example, the ending makes critics uncertain whether to take Stephen seriously or satirically, and the last section has generated a debate on "The Question of Esthetic Distance."[4] In contrast to Conrad's and Lawrence's willingness to take Garnett's reactions into account, Joyce absolutely refused to revise. Rather than attempt to cooperate with a publisher, Joyce terminated his agreement with Pinker a year later.

When B. W. Huebsch published *A Portrait* in 1916 in exactly the form Joyce had written it, the critical response was more favorable than Garnett had anticipated. Although some reviewers objected that the story was indeed sordid, the more frequent response was "recognition of his genius" (Magalaner and Kain 103). Praised for its originality and realism, the novel was a critical and commercial success. In 1918 Pound hailed it as "the nearest thing to Flaubertian prose" in English and took pride in its popularity:

> Despite the War, despite the paper shortage, and despite those old-established publishers whose god is their belly and whose god-father was the late F. T. Palgrave, there is a new edition of James Joyce's *A Portrait of the Artist as a Young Man*. It is extremely gratifying that this book should have "reached its fourth thousand," and the fact is significant in just so far as it marks the beginning of a new phase of English publishing, a phase comparable to that started in France some years ago by the *Mercure*. (Read 133)

Oblivious to the contradictions in his position, Pound complained that commercial publishers were mercenary while bragging about Joyce's sales. Like recent fiction that has entered the canon, *A Portrait* was praised by highbrow critics and bought by a viable public.

Since Joyce had been unable to publish *Dubliners* or *A Portrait* until 1914, public support came too late to affect his writing. Discovering that a single word could provoke censorship, he abandoned his original audience and his original aesthetic aims while writing *Ulysses*. Deprived of critical or popular feedback, he harbored an image of himself as a martyr to his art, persecuted by philistines on Publishers Row. He used this pose to justify his increasing absorption in questions of style. Joyce's earlier books had been written for a wide public, and *A Portrait* generated critical acclaim as well as commercial success. In contrast, *Ulysses* addressed an avant-garde audience. Although it was also bought by people who could not read it but who wanted to be part of a coterie, its narrative form stipulated a restricted audience.

Dubliners and *A Portrait* conform to the paradigm of impersonality Flaubert established. By the time *Dubliners* appeared, highbrow readers were familiar with this narrative perspective. For the most part, the first sections of *Ulysses* continue the free indirect discourse that Pound described: "Joyce's characters not only speak their own language, but they think their own language" (Read 195). When Pound praised *Ulysses* for conforming to Flaubert's model of impersonality, he ignored the ways the later sections departed from the conventional art novel and from his own objective of direct presentation. These sections make new demands on readers.

In *Joyce's Voices,* Hugh Kenner attributes the difficulty of *Ulysses* to Joyce's departure from the conventions of Flaubert's free indirect discourse. The narrative begins to veer away from any character's point of view; style supersedes syntax. Specific linguistic styles are no longer tethered to specific characters; instead, the "language is what we now confront" (41). Kenner argues that while pursuing Flaubert's ideal of "Objectivity," Joyce made a series of discoveries that led elsewhere. Joyce learned not only that *"the narrative idiom need not be the narrator's"* (18), but also that *"when statements can have no substance they can only have style"* (55). If the narrative voice could adopt any form of diction and syntax, it could also present a way of "writing about someone much as that someone would choose to be written about" (21). Kenner identifies "Sirens" as the turning point in Joyce's method and notes that Pound disapproved of the new style: "But with the eleventh episode, called 'Sirens,' something changed, and so radically that the author's staunchest advocate, Ezra Pound, was dismayed. (Would these events really lose, Pound wrote to ask, by being told in 'simple Maupassant'?) . . . Our immediate awareness now is of screens of language, through or past which it is not easy to see" (41). When style represents neither the narrator nor any character, it varies according to principles Joyce invited critics to identify for readers.

Free-floating styles are not the only reason *Ulysses* is difficult. Analyzing narrative form through a hypothetical reader's response, Wolfgang Iser identifies additional obstacles Joyce introduces:

> By constantly changing the perspective through the eighteen chapters, he draws attention to the normative pressure caused by the modes of observation inherent in any one style, thus revealing the extreme one-sidedness of each individual "act of interpretation." While the change of styles shows up these limitations, the process is underlined in the individual chapters by the surplus of nonintegrated, unstructured material. . . . And . . . in addition to these two factors, there is even a kind of authorial commentary which has these very limitations as its subject. (202)

Too many points of view, too much information, and an obfuscating narrator force the reader to make decisions authors ordinarily make. Joyce violates the assumption that the author will provide a "hierarchical organization of details" (Rabinowitz 53). The reader must select what is worth interpreting.[5]

Joyce knew *Ulysses* required guides. Kenner observes that Joyce

divided the usual tasks of authorship between himself and his expli-
cators. He produced the text and then arranged for them to provide
an exegesis. With careful coaching, Valery Larbaud, Stuart Gilbert,
and Frank Budgen provided the critical framework that has virtu-
ally become part of the text: "It was they, at his behest, who
equipped the great affirmation of meaninglessness with meaning. We
have been carrying on their work ever since . . ." (Kenner 63). For
example, Joyce deleted the Homeric chapter headings that appear
in the manuscript (Kenner 59), allowing his exegetes to provide
them, yet these titles are routinely cited as if they appeared in the
text.

Unlike late Victorian writers, Joyce circumvented the need to
build an audience because he attracted patrons. In the absence of a
commercial reading public, he depended on his patrons for the
approval sales ordinarily conveyed. Patronage included a Civil List
Grant of £100 secured partly by Yeats. Joyce told him the money
was "very encouraging as a sign of recognition" (*Selected Letters* 221).
He also sold manuscripts to the American collector John Quinn, a
patron of Conrad. He received money from the American heiress
Mrs. Harold McCormick, and eventually private presses vied for the
privilege of publishing *Work in Progress*. Although he earned a living by writing, he regretted that his audience was a coterie. He joked
about his meager public: "sometimes I find it difficult to keep my
eyes open—like the readers of my masterpieces" (*Selected Letters* 228),
and advised his "six or seven readers" to be content with *A Portrait*
and *Exiles* until he could finish *Ulysses* (*Selected Letters* 221). But he
wrote more seriously to a Swiss writer who had reviewed *A Portrait*:
"I envy anyone who writes in French not so much because I envy
the resources of that language . . . but on account of the public to
which one can appeal. Writing in English is the most ingenious tor-
ture ever devised for sins committed in previous lives. The English
reading public explains the reason why" (*Selected Letters* 230). Loss of
a wide public was the price he paid for freedom.[6]

Censorship made Joyce's work an avant-garde cause. The amateur publishers who eventually produced his books were eager to
take a stand against conventional society, but they were not able to
offer editorial advice. Patrons gave him truly unfettered freedom, and

Joyce began to depend on their unquestioning support for whatever he might write. The final, most complex sections of *Ulysses* and all of *Finnegans Wake* were written with the knowledge that he did not need to please an editor. Harriet Shaw Weaver, his principal benefactor, supported him handsomely from 1914 until his death. In addition to publishing *A Portrait* in *The Egoist,* Miss Weaver, as Joyce invariably addressed her, provided a regular and unconditional income that financed his independence of commercial publishers. She enabled him to "afford" the attitude Grant Richards condemned.

Not literary perspicacity but moral commitment inspired her patronage. Harriet Weaver became interested in Joyce's work as a result of Pound's reports of Joyce's publishing troubles; his cause stirred her sympathy. She decided to help him before she developed an appreciation of his work. Like many other supporters of modernist art, she admired Joyce for violating social and literary convention. The incongruity between her prim demeanor and Joyce's work startled her friends, but her biographers argue that she chose to help Joyce and others because they demonstrated a trait she lacked:

> the sense that a life of independent, creative action was still open before them. James Joyce and Dora Marsden had this appeal for her, and it was all the stronger because she never ceased to feel rebuked by their courage in cutting themselves off from conventional life. (Lidderdale 183)

Harriet Weaver's support of both Joyce and Dora Marsden illustrates the vagaries of patronage. Literary history has vindicated one choice but not the other. Too modest to feel qualified to advise any writer, Harriet Weaver limited her role to providing unquestioning support. This was exactly the kind of patron Joyce wanted. But while such patronage certainly increased Joyce's ability to write his books, it also contributed to the public's inability to read them. Joyce enjoyed the freedom this system permitted, but he lost the editorial advice that formerly mediated between authors and readers. The ideology of the unfettered artist treats this loss as an advantage, but editing is not inherently oppressive. It can provide a valuable early response, as Joyce himself knew. Although literary judgment did not inspire Miss Weaver's patronage, Joyce chose to regard her support as confirmation of the literary value of his work. He thanked her for both her generosity and her encouragement (*Selected Letters* 224).

While writing *Ulysses* Joyce took pains to explain his intention to Harriet Weaver and other correspondents. He was annoyed when they failed to comprehend him, but he blamed them, not himself, for the problem. Resorting to Flaubert's argument that laborious composition was a sign of value, he defended the "Sirens" episode to Miss Weaver: "Since the receipt of your letter I have read this chapter again several times. It took me five months to write it and always when I have finished an episode my mind lapses into a state of blank apathy out of which it seems that neither I nor the wretched book will ever more emerge" (*Selected Letters* 240). Joyce owed Harriet Weaver a respectful explanation because of her patronage; she may not have been entitled to critical respect. Pound, however, was a more complex case. His initial enthusiasm for Joyce had brought both critical attention and Miss Weaver's support. Pound was the quintessential modernist, prepared by erudition and iconoclasm to appreciate Joyce's latest work, yet even he found it too esoteric.

Joyce perceived that Pound's own art interfered with the attention he was willing to give someone else's demanding work: "Mr Pound wrote to me rather hastily in disapproval but I think that his disapproval is based on grounds which are not legitimate and is due chiefly to the varied interests of his admirable and energetic artistic life" (*Selected Letters* 240). Determined to be as arcane as he chose, each demanded readers who were willing to follow the text's clues to hidden associations. Contemporary cultural and literary traditions could not provide an adequate context for construing these works; they required extended study. Reconstructing the unique network of associations in each writer's psyche, critics provided keys to their texts, but the possibility of an unmediated rhetorical effect was lost. Both Joyce and Pound found such critics, but they did not find this kind of interest among fellow artists. Joyce complained: "Not a soul to talk to about Bloom. Lent the chapter to one or two people but they know as much about it as the parliamentary side of my arse" (*Selected Letters* 246). He wanted readers, but he wanted them only on his own terms: they would need to retrace each step of his thinking.

In Bernard Benstock's words, "Joyce refused to stoop to conquer although he certainly hoped to please" (223).

Whether or not he had readers, Joyce now had buyers. *Ulysses* was in demand as soon as it was banned. Before critical opinion could form, *Ulysses* became a *succès de scandale* when installments appeared in *The Little Review* in 1918. B. W. Huebsch, a New York publisher who also sold Lawrence's banned books, proposed a private edition of one thousand copies at Fr 150 each (*Selected Letters* 272), though he withdrew his offer when *The Little Review* was suppressed. Sylvia Beach produced a second edition of two thousand copies of *Ulysses* at £2.2.0 a copy which sold out in four days (*Selected Letters* 292). Unable to publish legally, Joyce could not prevent Samual Roth from pirating the book. Printing monthly installments, Roth sold forty thousand copies a month (*Selected Letters* 315).

Again thanks to Pound, Joyce found another patron in Sylvia Beach. Taking an interest in his difficulties, she proposed publishing *Ulysses* by subscription in Paris. Like Harriet Weaver, Sylvia Beach was an incongruous publisher of "obscene" literature. She was a minister's daughter, and her manner was thoroughly respectable. She too disclaimed any literary expertise: "I think they let me read [their manuscripts] because I never criticized them. . . . They had too much talent for me to pass judgment on anything they wrote" (Ford 30). Beach's 1922 edition was an immediate success. There were not enough copies to meet the demand: "Since the announcement that the book was out the shop has been in a state of siege—buyers driving up two or three times a day and no copies to give them. . . . A more nerveracking conclusion to the history of the book could scarcely have been imagined!" (*Selected Letters* 288). Joyce appreciated the irony of his underground popularity:

> On the material side I think if the edition goes well (subscriptions come every day—three today from Australia) I will receive between 100,000 and 150,000 [lire]. But that is not what concerns me. No sum of money could compensate me for my toil. . . . Something really comic could be written about the subscribers to my tome—a son or nephew of Bela Kun, the British Minister of War Winston Churchill, an Anglican bishop and a leader of the Irish revolutionary movement.

I have become a monument—no, a vespasian [i.e., urinal]. (*Selected Letters* 281n)

After *Ulysses* became a sensation, commercial publishers eagerly sought Joyce's work. In 1927 the young firm of Boni and Liveright offered $2,000 and 15 percent royalties for *Finnegans Wake,* but Joyce held out for better terms (*Selected Letters* 323). In 1932 he accepted a bid from Bennett Cerf at Random House for *Ulysses.* In the meantime, two American publishers offered an advance of $11,000 and 20 percent royalties on *Finnegans Wake* which he did not accept.[7] His income increased substantially when the American ban on *Ulysses* was lifted in 1933, thanks to Cerf's efforts. Justice John M. Woolsey's decision in that case reaffirmed the dichotomy between art and money when he ruled that *Ulysses* was not obscene because it was too difficult to have been written for profit.

Once *Ulysses* established Joyce's position as the paramount modernist artist, he was free to write whatever he wished. In Pierre Bourdieu's terms, he had accumulated enough cultural capital to live off its interest. He invested everything in *Finnegans Wake,* but his most loyal advocates questioned the wisdom of this decision. *Ulysses* abandons the convention that language distinguishes individual characters from one another; *Finnegans Wake* departs from natural language altogether, and its intelligibility has been debated since it appeared.

Joyce's ultimate rhetorical stance amounted to domination of the reader's life, his final revenge. He called his last book a "wordspiderweb" to trap his prey (*Selected Letters* 393n). He admitted, "The demand that I make of my reader . . . is that he should devote his whole life to reading my works" (Ellmann 703). He wrote *Finnegans Wake* for "that ideal reader suffering from an ideal insomnia" (Ellmann 703). Whatever irony Joyce intended in these remarks, they accurately described the effect of the text on readers. The book baffled Pound: "I will have another go at it, but up to present I make nothing of it whatever. Nothing so far as I make out, nothing short of divine vision or a new cure for the clapp can possibly be worth all that circumambient peripherization" (Ellmann 584). Pound considered it unreadable, "In his view the author of *Work in Progress* was 'in regress'" (Ellmann 585). Although Harriet Weaver continued to support Joyce financially, she told him, "It seems to me you are wasting your genius" (Ellmann 590).

While modernist authors were unable to appreciate one another's work because they were immersed in their own writing, many potential readers were unwilling to devote themselves to discipleship. H. G. Wells spoke for the reader's rights and the social function of art in a letter to Joyce. Although Wells admired the intricacy of *Finnegans Wake,* he argued that Joyce's demands on the reader were excessive:

> It's a considerable thing because you are a very considerable man and you have in your crowded composition a mighty genius for expression which has escaped discipline. But I don't think it gets anywhere. You have turned your back on common men, on their elementary needs and their restricted time and intelligence and you have elaborated. What is the result? Vast riddles. Your last two works have been more amusing and exciting to write than they will ever be to read. (Ellmann 608)

Finding Joyce's pleasure in composition incommensurate with the reader's pleasure in reading, Wells phrased his objections as a defense of the common man. His argument also accounts for the avant-garde readers who supported Joyce because his prose required unrestricted quantities of time and intelligence.

Confronted with incomprehension, Joyce invoked a mimetic defense. He was incoherent because night thoughts were incoherent:

> In writing of the night, I really could not, I felt I could not, use words in their ordinary connections. Used that way they do not express how things are in the night, in the different stages—conscious, then semi-conscious, then unconscious. I found that it could not be done with words in their ordinary relations and connections. When morning comes of course everything will be clear again. . . . I'll give them back their English language. I'm not destroying it for good. (Ellmann 546)

He expected readers to recognize their own experience in his rendering of night thoughts.

Joyce was also driven to the work-value defense he had used for *Ulysses:* "They cannot understand it. Therefore they say it is meaningless. Now if it were meaningless it could be written quickly, without thought, without pains, without erudition; but I assure you that these twenty pages now before us cost me twelve hundred hours and an enormous expense of spirit" (Ellmann 598). Justifying his book entirely in terms of its meaning to him and the effort it cost him, Joyce mentioned no rhetorical aims.

In addition, a desire to mystify readers lay beneath Joyce's defenses. Stanislaus Joyce, a perceptive if not impartial critic of his brother's work, suggested that Joyce's obscurity was the result of his ambivalence about releasing his work for publication. Apart from artistic integrity, Stanislaus located a motive for formal difficulty in the use of autobiographical material: "Jim is thought to be very frank about himself but his style is such that it might be contended that he confesses in a foreign language—an easier confession than in the vulgar tongue" (Ellmann 148). If Joyce wanted to reveal and conceal his meaning simultaneously, an inaccessible style limited his audience to disciples committed to penetrating its secrets.

Joyce provided Harriet Weaver with explanatory keys, but he did not respond to her concern for the reader's quandary:

> without comprehensive key and glossary, such as you very kindly made out for me, the poor hapless reader loses a very great deal of your intention; flounders, helplessly, is in imminent danger, in fact, of being as totally lost to view as that illfated vegetation you mentioned. Perhaps you wish him, her and them to disappear from the horizon in this way—and in particular all officials—so that at least the book itself may float across safely to that far shore of "Doublin all the time." (Ellmann 584)

Perceiving hostility to readers behind the obscurity of the text, Miss Weaver expressed a publisher's usual concern for the reader's interests, but she did not impose her opinion.

Joyce offered readers indirect assistance, as he had with *Ulysses*. He helped his friends write critical guides. Choosing his own "twelve apostles," he organized *Our Exagmination round His Factification for Incamination of Work in Progress* to aid readers. Recognizing the value of his reputation, Joyce also tried to arrange an authorized biography. He approached Stuart Gilbert, who declined, refusing to share

Joyce's sense of martyrdom. Gilbert told him, "You're a very lucky man. You have money, fame, a family" (Ellmann 631). Joyce then turned to Herbert Gorman. Ellmann remarks, "Without saying so to Gorman directly, he made clear that he was to be treated as a saint with an unusually protracted martyrdom" (631).

Whether or not Pound and Miss Weaver were correct in regarding *Finnegans Wake* as a waste of Joyce's talent, the fact that such a book was published and bought indicates the impact of an author's position in the literary field. Joyce's prestige made it a valuable property. After sections appeared in *transatlantic review* in 1924, he received requests to publish extracts in *transition, Contact Collection* (Paris), *Navire d'Argent, This Quarter,* and Eliot's *Criterion.* Harry and Caresse Crosby achieved what "was now the aim of all private presses, to publish an excerpt from *Work in Progress*" (Ellmann 614) when Joyce gave them *Tales Told of Shem and Shaun* for their Black Sun Press. Sections were also published by Crosby Gaige and Faber and Faber. Sylvia Beach expected to publish the complete *Finnegans Wake,* but other offers emerged. B. W. Huebsch secured it for the Viking Press in 1931, though it was not finished until 1938. It was finally published in 1939 and has remained in print.

Like other modernists, Joyce saw that *succès de scandale* contributed to *succès d'estime,* but he resented this kind of attention: "In practically no case has any consideration shown to my work since its appearance been uninfluenced by the general impression 'il semble avoir très réussi' which I purposely tried to keep to set off other elements of the case" (*Selected Letters* 327).[8] Illicit acclaim was not the response Joyce sought: he still wanted to be read in Ireland. Although he was able to support himself and his family through his art and also was able to practice his art in a state close to unfettered freedom, his work did not produce the effect he sought on his original target, the Irish people. When Yeats invited him to join the Academy of Irish Letters, he refused to allow his name to be connected with such an organization (*Selected Letters* 365).

Although Joyce's patrons objected to its impenetrability, a small group of readers defended *Finnegans Wake* as a symbol of the artist's creative freedom. The difficulty of the text stipulated its audience, and people eager to belong to the avant-garde rushed to join his coterie. Joyce experienced the then rare phenomenon of acclaim without appreciation. His most literate critics regretted that his work was incomprehensible, and his most enthusiastic fans bought it because it was. Robert McAlmon, an American writer and private publisher who knew Joyce in Paris, mocked the expatriate audience which idolized Joyce yet could not understand his work (314). Joyce saw this irony too but persisted because he connected his private vision with artistic integrity; to simplify for the reader would be an aesthetic compromise.

Joyce attributed his publishing troubles to readers' personal animosity toward him. Late in his life, he still blamed his failure to find a public on readers' resentment:

> I described the people and the conditions in my country; I reproduced certain city types of a certain social level. They didn't forgive me for it. Some grudged my not concealing what I had seen, others were annoyed because of my way of expressing myself, which they didn't understand at all. In short, some were enraged by the realistic picture, others by the style. They all took revenge. (Ellmann 689)

Projecting his own desire for revenge onto an indifferent public, Joyce ignored the legal issues his early fiction raised and the difficulty of his later work. Maintaining his stance as a martyr, he felt he was not responsible for his troubles, and in a sense he was right. It is hard to imagine that Joyce could have recast his writing to meet a commercial publisher's requirements if Harriet Weaver had not appeared. Responding to her doubts about *Ulysses*, Joyce told her: "I confess that it is an extremely tiresome book but it is the only book which I am able to write at present" (*Selected Letters* 241). Although he attributed this compulsion to artistic integrity, the conflict between ideologies of the artist and the professional also contributed to his intransigence.

The patronage of an avant-garde coterie both through grants and private presses not only supported Joyce's obscurity but encouraged it. Independent of market constraints, Joyce allowed his art to approach the limit of intelligibility. He could be contemptuous of readers' responses, while commercial publishers from Grant Richards on could not "afford" this attitude until Joyce's reputation made the accessibility of his writing unimportant. Patronage allowed Joyce's early rhetoric of revenge to dissipate in word play. Caught in the embrace of an avant-garde readership, Joyce sacrificed the Irish public he had once sought.

CHAPTER FOUR

D. H. Lawrence: Impersonality and the Unconscious

Like other modernists, D. H. Lawrence inherited contradictory
models of authorship. He was deeply alienated from society yet committed to reforming it. He was contemptuous of the mass audience
yet dependent on the income it provided. He believed in the truth
of his own experience yet tried to be impersonal. Evidence for each
pole of these dichotomies appears in biographies and in his letters,
but most critics emphasize the facts that conform to the plot of the
unfettered artist rather than that of the professional author. Like
Kundera's readers of Goethe and Hemingway, critics persistently
interpret Lawrence's fiction as a reflection of his life (Arcana). In their
accounts, the less attention Lawrence paid to theories of art or the
demands of publishers, the better he fit their idea of the natural
genius. Although Lawrence attributed his early work to spontaneous
feeling, critics who emphasize this Romantic model of authorship
neglect the development of his artistry as well as his professionalism.
Lawrence's work is exceptionally autobiographical, but it also evokes
such a strong response in readers that it has been prosecuted as
pornography.

Lawrence's interest in the unconscious reinforces his reputation
as a natural writer. Although psychoanalytic theory was an important
factor in the modernist critique of nineteenth-century fiction and its
psychology, the Freudian unconscious revitalized the Romantic

model of the expressive artist. In both Romantic and psychoanalytic models, the value of art depends on the depth of its source, and the unconscious is even more powerful and mysterious than emotion. Like deep feeling, the unconscious seems to belong to the author's personal life rather than to any conscious aesthetic or rhetorical goal.

If Lawrence's work owes its success to the strength of his unconscious, as many critics argue, evidence that he was a conscious craftsman and a professional author seeking sales would only contaminate the purity of his art. While this line of reasoning is strongest in biographies of Lawrence, it also influences other kinds of criticism, not only because his fiction corresponds to events in his life, but also because the tension between conscious and unconscious behavior is a pervasive theme in his work. His interest in the unconscious encourages readers to assume that his writing was also produced unconsciously.

Lawrence's idea of the unconscious did not develop naturally. Frieda Weekley introduced him to psychoanalytic theory. Although he objected to some of Freud's ideas, depth psychology helped Lawrence make his work more impersonal by showing him general patterns in his own experience. As he gained distance from the autobiographical source of his material, his technical control increased. Thus, his knowledge of Freud's theory of the unconscious contributed to the modernist form of his fiction.

In addition to psychoanalytic theory, Lawrence's publishing experiences pushed him toward modernism. Editors introduced him to Flaubert's ideals of impersonality and formal control, and in his apprenticeship, Lawrence accepted their advice. Thanks to several editors, he learned to avoid extravagant description, contrived plots, and unconvincing characterization. After his first two novels attracted serious critical attention, the publication of *Sons and Lovers* in 1913 created a sensation; *The Rainbow* and *Women in Love* soon followed. Harry T. Moore expresses the critical consensus on these books: "For, although he often wrote magnificently during the rest of his life, he never again, despite his increasing skill in the use of language, achieved the integration of art and idea that he manifested in *The Rainbow* and *Women in Love*" (*Priest of Love* 272). Undermining this triumphant debut, the government's suppression of *The Rainbow* in 1915 and publishers' subsequent rejections of *Women in Love* shook Lawrence's confidence in his audience, and his writing changed.

Corroborating evidence in his letters, the narrative point of view in his novels indicates Lawrence's conception of his reader at various stages of his career. When he believed readers had a "need" for his work (Boulton 2:171), he used what he called an "intimate" style (Boulton 3:549).[1] This style is impersonal in allowing the narrator's voice to merge with the language of various characters yet is intimate in penetrating characters' unconscious feelings. Like Flaubert's free indirect discourse, Lawrence's "intimate" style avoids an intrusive narrator and consistently focalizes the narrative from various characters' positions. But whereas Flaubert scrupulously limited the third person narrator's knowledge to a character's thoughts, allowing only the effects of the unconscious to appear, Lawrence required an omniscient narrator to explore the dynamics of what remained unconscious. To convey unconscious experience, he resurrected the omniscient narrator in a new guise. This omniscient yet impersonal point of view is used in *Sons and Lovers, The Rainbow, Women in Love,* and *Lady Chatterley's Lover.* The narrators of these novels use stylistic devices such as extended metaphor, repetition, rhythm, alliteration, and contradiction to create symbolic scenes that convey unconscious experience. Conforming to modernist criteria of impersonality and experimental form, these novels have become the Lawrence canon.

The fiction Lawrence wrote as an expatriate in the 1920s, however, departs from modernist form. After censorship deprived him of his audience, Lawrence was in the rhetorical position of postmodernists, and the novels of this period resemble postmodernist fiction in their disregard for impersonality. Isolated from his readers, Lawrence anticipated postmodernists in his use of an intrusive first-person narrator (except in *The Plumed Serpent*) who speaks in his own voice, commenting freely on the characters, the plot, and the artificial structure of fiction. Through apostrophe, the narrator inscribes in the text the reader he no longer takes for granted. Freed from the conventions of impersonality, works such as *The Lost Girl, Mr Noon, Aaron's Rod, Kangaroo,* and *The Plumed Serpent* fit not modernist but postmodernist criteria. Read in this context, the novels of this period begin to look less like bad fiction and more like metafiction.

Lawrence made contradictory statements about his rhetorical intentions.[2] Like Conrad, he initially expected no conflict between sales and acclaim. He wanted a wide audience and a good income from all his work; Jessie Chambers remembers him as a novice exclaiming, "I'll make two thousand a year!" (Worthen, *Idea* 4). But his departure from England in 1920 confirmed the complaints of estrangement from readers he reiterated in his letters from 1920 to 1926. Not until he found a way to reach readers directly through private publication did he recover his conviction that his work would find the audience he sought. He began *Lady Chatterley's Lover,* his most personal and most didactic book, only when he was certain it would be published as written. This novel resembles his earlier canonical work because he once again felt he was addressing an immediate need in his audience.

A reexamination of Lawrence's career in terms of his conception of his audience shows that both aesthetic and commercial aims contributed to the quality of his writing; neither detracted from it. Although many critics correlate his canonical work with what they consider the uninhibited expression of his unconscious, it is also possible to show that these novels were written when he was working toward Flaubertian standards of impersonality and trying to expand his audience. His least admired fiction was written when he felt isolated, both as a novice and in the 1920s when he withdrew from the audience he had built. Although Flaubert conceived of impersonality as a way to make art autonomous, Lawrence found that impersonal form brought him closer to readers. It offered an escape from confinement in the subjective self, and it was a sign of professional competence. Inspiration seemed erratic and amateurish compared to the control and reliability of Flaubert's model of craftsmanship. Imposing distance between his own life and his work, impersonality brought his art closer to his audience. Thus, both conscious formal control and attention to readers' responses distinguish his modernist novels from the freer fiction of the 1920s.

Lawrence's earliest statements of intention echoed Romantic assertions that the value of art depended on the intensity of the artist's feeling rather than on the fullness of the reader's response. He was thoroughly Romantic in insisting that emotion generated form organically and spontaneously. In 1908 he claimed that "an unconscious artist often puts the wrong words to the right feeling. So long as the feeling's right, it doesn't matter so much" (Boulton 1:102). At this point, his idea of the unconscious artist seems to suggest no more than an intuitive confidence. His faith in sincerity rather than skill allowed him to defend feeling over form. In 1912 he rephrased the aestheticist shibboleth, "Art for art's sake," to reaffirm the connection between art and the artist's life: "I always say, my motto is 'Art for my sake'. If I *want* to write, I write—and if I don't want to, I won't. The difficulty is to find exactly the form one's passion—work is produced by passion with me, like kisses—is it with you?—wants to take" (Boulton 1:491). The narcissism of his "motto" is reinforced by the erotic image of work being like kisses. In the Romantic tradition of the expressive poet, Lawrence judged form by its fidelity to its emotional source and simply assumed it would inevitably produce a sympathetic response in the reader. Nevertheless, he showed his early writing to women he knew and responded to their comments in his revisions.

Having let "passion" produce his first work, Lawrence was reluctant to risk rejection. Revealing a common source of hostility to publishers, he agonized over an editor's response: "Will he want it? This transacting of literary business makes me sick. I have no faith in myself at the end, and I simply loathe writing" (Boulton 1:161). Lawrence was objecting not to the particular judge but to the need to submit to anyone's judgment. Both his repugnance at selling his work and his sensitivity to criticism contributed to his distress.

His childhood friend, Jessie Chambers, took the decisive step of sending some of his poems to *The English Review*. The journal's managing editor, Ford Madox Hueffer, not only accepted the poems at once but also made himself Lawrence's mentor. Hueffer acted as agent in recommending Lawrence's first novel to William Heinemann. The publisher liked the manuscript of *The White Peacock* (1911) and offered Lawrence a contract, stipulating an option on his next novel. Although Heinemann accepted the manuscript, his editor, Sidney Pawling, required extensive revisions. Like novice authors of the preceding generation, Lawrence was pleased at Pawling's interest and accepted his advice: "A good deal of it, including the whole of the third part, I have re-written. To be sure, it needed it. I think I have removed all the offensive morsels, all the damns, the devils and the sweat" (Boulton 1:158). Indecency, however, was not the main objection; Pawling also asked him to condense the manuscript (Boulton 1:158). This professional advice did not destroy Lawrence's originality; it significantly improved the book.

Despite laborious editing and rewriting, many faults escaped correction. Reviewers praised descriptive passages, especially natural scenes, but objected to glaring structural weaknesses that remained.[3] The first-person narrator generates many of these faults.[4] Cyril, the narrator, cannot credibly present other characters' feelings, particularly when they are reacting to him. For example, when Cyril describes his friendship with George Saxton, a farmer's son, he unpersuasively records George's response to his tutelage:

> I would give him the gist of what I knew of chemistry, and botany, and psychology. Day after day I told him what the professors had told me; of life, of sex and its origins; of Schopenhauer and William James. . . . Religion was nothing to him. So he heard all I had to say with an open mind, and understood the drift of things very rapidly, and quickly made these ideas part of himself. (58)

Locked in his own point of view, Cyril reduces George to a pliant acolyte. In a later book, such a passage might have expressed George's resentment as well as his appreciation.

The first person is most awkward when Cyril attempts to render his own unconscious thoughts:

> I sat by my window and watched the low clouds reel and stagger past. It seemed as if everything were being swept along—I myself seemed to have lost my substance, to have become detached from concrete things and the firm trodden pavement of everyday life. (83)

Cyril's self-reported feelings can represent thought as a stream of consciousness but cannot go any deeper. As unconscious feeling became more prominent in his work, Lawrence abandoned the first-person narrator.

Pawling accepted Lawrence's first manuscript in spite of its narrative faults because he perceived its literary and commercial value.

From this point on, the only obstacle to publication Lawrence faced was censorship. He believed his frankness was far more moral than the evasions publishers requested, but publishers knew that certain passages were actionable. They also knew, however, that the eroticism in Lawrence's work would make it extremely profitable. Heinemann was reluctant to publish Lawrence's second novel, *The Trespasser* (still called "The Saga of Siegmund"), because it was "erotic," but he also wanted to prevent any other firm from bringing it out. Rather than refuse the book and thus lose his option, Heinemann tried to persuade Lawrence to withdraw it and submit another manuscript.

Warned that publication could permanently damage his reputation as a serious writer, Lawrence turned to Edward Garnett, then an editor at Duckworth, for advice:

> I shall like to hear your opinion of the work. Hueffer called it "a rotten work of genuis" [*sic*], but he was prejudiced against the inconsequential style; said that erotic literature must be in the form of high art.
>
> This Saga, on the contrary, is based on brief notes made from actuality. Nevertheless I swear it has true form. (Boulton 1:330)

Hueffer's comment anticipates the legal arguments against censorship of *Lady Chatterley's Lover:* if erotic literature is high art, it is not pornography. The unspoken assumption underlying the dichotomy of art and pornography is that money is the sign of vice. If erotic literature addresses an elite audience, it is art because it appears indifferent to profit. If it attracts a mass audience, however, it seems pornographic because it produces money.

Lawrence was caught in this contradiction. He wanted his novel to address a wide audience, but he certainly did not consider it pornographic. He defended it as realism and tried to link it to high art through its form. He began to see that too much feeling could be as harmful as too much form. He told Garnett *The Trespasser* was so personal that he cringed at publishing it:

> It is so much oneself, one's naked self. I give myself away so much, and write what is my most palpitant, sensitive self, that I loathe the book, because it will betray me to a parcel of fools. Which is what any deeply personal or lyrical writer feels, I guess. . . .

> I wish the Trespasser were to be issued privately, to a few folk
> who had understanding. But I suppose, by all the rules of life, it must
> take open chance, if it's good enough. (Boulton 1:353)

He realized autobiographical material added to his ambivalence about
publication. Hoping to reach a sympathetic audience, he also feared
readers' mockery.

Lawrence's desire to reduce this sense of exposure to an unknown
audience was another motive to move from self-expression to the
"accurate-impersonal school of Flaubert" (Boulton 1:169). Trying to
introduce his protégé to modernist aesthetics, Hueffer urged
Lawrence to adopt Flaubert's refinements of form. Lawrence disputed these ideas at first: "Hueffer wrote me this morning concern-
ing the second novel. He says it's a rotten work of genius, one fourth
of which is the stuff of masterpiece. He belongs to the opposite
school of novelists to me: he says prose *must* be impersonal, like
Turguenev or Flaubert. I say no" (Boulton 1:178). Hueffer's criticism must have stung him, however, because only a month later he
described his third novel in the exact terms Hueffer had taught him:
"Paul Morel will be a novel—not a florid prose poem, or a decorated
idyll running to seed in realism: but a restrained, somewhat impersonal novel. It interests me very much. I wish I were not so agitated
just now, and could do more" (Boulton 1:184).

Beginning with this novel, Lawrence's revisions made his fiction
more impersonal. At first, he defended "Paul Morel" against the criticism that it was too formless. He told Heinemann's editor:

> Now I know it's a good thing, even a bit great. . . . It's not so strongly
> concentric as the fashionable folk under French influence—you see
> I suffered badly from Hueffer re Flaubert and perfection—want it. It
> may seem loose—and I may cut the childhood part—if you think bet-
> ter so—and perhaps you'll want me to spoil some of the good stuff.
> But it is rather great. (Boulton 1:416–17)

The editor did not agree. He appealed to Lawrence on behalf of the
reader:

> I feel that the book is unsatisfactory from several points of view; not
> only because it lacks unity, without which the reader's interest can-
> not be held, but more so because its want of reticence makes it unfit,
> I fear, altogether for publication in England as things are. The tyranny

of the Libraries is such that a book far less out-spoken would certainly be damned (and there is practically no market for fiction outside of them). (Boulton 1:421n)

Fear of losing library sales was only part of his objection; he also felt the novel failed to create sympathy for any character—even Paul. The editor wrote Garnett to clarify his reaction: "But apart from this [indecency] altogether, I don't feel that the book as a whole comes up to Lawrence's real mark. It seems to me to need pulling together: it is not of a piece. But the real theme of the story is not arrived at till half way through" (Boulton 1:424n). Although these objections made Lawrence angry, he followed the editor's advice: "And Heinemann, I can see, is quite right, as a business man" (Boulton 1:422). Unwilling to accept the criticism on aesthetic grounds, he discredited it as an opinion tainted by commercial judgment.

Lawrence's cooperation with publishers is a problem for his biographers. Since modernism has been defined as autonomous and antirhetorical, Lawrence's explicit statements of rhetorical intention undercut his status as an artist. To defend Lawrence, some biographers try to minimize his concern with form and readers. Harry T. Moore illustrates this tendency in *The Priest of Love*. After recounting the events that led to the publication of *Sons and Lovers* and detailing the slow process of revision and Lawrence's gradual control of form, Moore disregards his own evidence. He records Lawrence's statements of intention but contradicts them:

> When Lawrence finished the last draft, he wrote to his adviser, "I tell you it has got form—*form:* haven't I made it patiently, out of sweat as well as blood"—but the sweat and blood did not come from Lawrence's struggle with "form" so much as from his sufferings at reliving the past. For this deeper, more vital reworking of the manuscript demanded a greater intensification of the past than the earlier versions had. Authors often try to shake off burdens of the past by writing about it. Sometimes the process is conscious, sometimes not: its effectiveness usually depends upon the strength and depth of the feeling involved. (163)

To attribute this "sweat and blood" to the psychological process of "reliving the past," Moore dismisses Lawrence's stated rhetorical aim of improving the form.

Like other modern biographers, Moore easily assimilates psycho-analytic valorization of the unconscious to the Romantic idea that deep feeling is the source of art. Conscious technique violates both principles. Moore regards writing as a form of therapy that releases pent up feelings. Lawrence himself felt this way after writing *Sons and Lovers:* "But one sheds ones [*sic*] sicknesses in books—repeats and presents again ones emotions, to be master of them" (Boulton 2:90). Writing may be, as Wordsworth put it, the "timely utterance" that gives the author some relief, but this personal struggle does not account for the rhetorical effect of the text on readers.

An author's conscious control of form does not block readers' unconscious responses. In "Creative Writers and Day-Dreaming," Freud describes the relationship between the source of art in the writer's unconscious and the writer's technical skill. Freud distin-guishes art from day-dreaming on the basis of form; the writer "bribes" the audience with a formal, aesthetic pleasure to make his or her fantasies pleasurable for the reader (153). This diversion is nec-essary to release the unconscious tensions in the reader's mind:

> The writer . . . bribes us by the purely formal—that is aesthetic—yield of pleasure which he offers us in the presentation of his phantasies. . . . In my opinion, all the aesthetic pleasure which a creative writer affords us has the character of a fore-pleasure of this kind, and our actual enjoyment of an imaginative work proceeds from a liberation of tensions in our minds. It may even be that not a little of this effect is due to the writer's enabling us thenceforward to enjoy our own day-dreams without self-reproach or shame. (153)

In Freud's model, the author's conscious control of formal elements *increases* the possibility that the reader's unconscious will respond to the text.

Like the cultural dichotomy between art and money, the aes-thetic assumption that unconscious writing is pure while conscious control is venal has obscured Lawrence's rhetorical intentions. Early psychoanalytic critics were particularly eager to establish the uncon-scious origin of his work. Turning to literature for scientific evi-dence, they sought representations of characters untainted by prior knowledge of Freud. Finding *Sons and Lovers* an exemplary text, Alfred Booth Kuttner as early as 1916 argued that because literature reflects life, it provides a source of evidence for psychoanalytic theory:

> [*Sons and Lovers*] ranks high, very high as a piece of literature and at the same time it embodies a theory which it illustrates and exemplifies with a completeness that is nothing less than astonishing. Fortunately there can be no doubt as to the authenticity of the author's inspiration. For it would be fatal if the novel had been written with the express purpose of illustrating a theory: it would, by that very admission, be worthless as a proof of that theory. (77)

Kuttner conflates inspiration and the unconscious as signs of authenticity. If Lawrence had consciously shaped the novel to conform to Freud's ideas, it would be spoiled for science. Kuttner's rhetorical theory reverses Freud's model. Whereas Freud says the conscious artist arouses the unconscious response of the reader, Kuttner claims the unconscious artist evokes the reader's conscious response:

> For a new truth about ourselves, which may seem altogether grotesque and impossible when presented to us as an arid theory, often gains unexpected confirmation when presented to us in a powerful work of literature as an authentic piece of life. (77)

Literature, for Kuttner, displays in characters what we wish to conceal from ourselves. In contrast to Freud's model, Kuttner's mimetic model of literature as a mirror that presents an authentic image does not account for the artist's conscious control of form or rhetorical intention.

Despite critics' predilection for an emotional, inspired, or unconscious source of art, editorial advice helped Lawrence develop formal control. In *The Priest of Love,* Moore acknowledges the extent of Garnett's influence: the manuscript of *Sons and Lovers* "shows how severe Edward Garnett was in making excisions from it for the published version" (389). First, for the sake of decency, Lawrence gave Garnett permission to cut as he saw fit:

> Have I made those naked scenes in Paul Morel tame enough. You cut them if you like. Yet they are so clean—and I *have* patiently and laboriously constructed that novel. (Boulton 1:478)

Second, for the sake of form, he allowed Garnett to reduce it one-tenth to improve its pace:

> I sit in sadness and grief after your letter. I daren't say anything. All
> right, take out what you think necessary. (Boulton 1:481)

Distressed at the need to revise, he conceded that changes were necessary. Between rejection in July 1912 and final publication in 1913, Lawrence rewrote *Sons and Lovers* extensively. When his pride recovered from the initial criticism, Lawrence thanked Garnett for conveying his opinion: "Thanks very much for the notes on P[aul] M[orel]. I agree with all you say, and will do all I can" (Boulton 1:426).

The most significant external influence on *Sons and Lovers* came from Frieda Weekley, who eloped with Lawrence in 1912. She and her sister were part of an intellectual circle in Germany that was close to Freud.[5] She had been the mistress of Otto Gross, a physician who was one of Freud's earliest colleagues. This connection made it possible for her to discuss psychoanalytic theory and practice with Lawrence before translations of Freud's writings made them known in England. By introducing Lawrence to Freud's theories, however unsystematically, she gave him a way to reconcile autobiographical material with the modernist aesthetic of impersonality. When he recognized psychoanalytic themes in his story, he was able to impose conscious control on a book about unconscious feelings. Thus, Paul's Oedipal characteristics, which are pivotal in the debate about Freud's influence, can be traced to Lawrence's rhetorical intentions as well as to biographical sources.

The terms of the debate on the extent of Freud's effect on Lawrence's work reflect the ideological opposition between expressive art and rhetoric. Frederick J. Hoffman notes:

> Lawrence caught Frieda's enthusiasm for "things German" almost
> immediately. . . . Before the final draft was ready for the publishers,
> perhaps during the time of revision, Lawrence was listening to
> Frieda's explanations of Freud and arguing with her about Freud's
> contribution to modern thought. "Yes, Lawrence knew about Freud
> before he wrote the final draft of *Sons and Lovers,*" Frieda tells me in
> a letter of November 21, 1942. (103–4)

Hoffman concedes that "Lawrence may have increased the emphasis in the novel upon the mother-son relationship, to the neglect of other matters, and given it the striking clarity which it enjoys in the published book," yet he immediately denies its importance in favor of an expressive theory of art: "But the relationship was there long before Lawrence's final revision; and he did not allow any clinical or psychological commentary to interfere with the literary excellence of the novel as a whole" (104).

Like Hoffman, H. M. Daleski acknowledges and then discounts Frieda Weekley's testimony:

> [B]ut I am inclined to accept Hoffman's conclusion that "it is doubt-ful . . . that the revision of *Sons and Lovers* was more than superficially affected by Lawrence's introduction to psychoanalysis." At that time Lawrence's knowledge of Freudian theory was derived at second-hand from Frieda, and she probably did no more than confirm his intuitive apprehension of the nature of Paul's relations with his par-ents. Nor does the book betray any signs of artificial grafting. (33)

Daleski wants to preserve Lawrence's "intuitive," or unconscious, apprehension from even "second-hand" theorizing: "From the out-set he has a clear understanding of the nature of Paul's love for his mother and his hatred of his father" (30). Like Kuttner, Hoffman and Daleski assume that if Lawrence had consciously used Freudian theory, he would have compromised his art. For all three critics, conscious use of a theory corrupts direct expression of experience. Daleski prefers to demean Frieda Weekley's influence as superficial rather than accept the evidence of Lawrence's extensive revision that successive drafts provide.

The ideology that art must be produced spontaneously and unconsciously is so pervasive that critics who perceive the extent of Freud's influence attribute the novel's faults to Freud's ideas. For example, Daniel A. Weiss criticizes descriptions of Gertrude Morel as "mechanically collated evidence of the Oedipal relationship" (112). Mark Spilka finds evidence of two psychologies, Lawrence's and Freud's: "So Lawrence may well have written the book, at first, in accord with his own developing psychology, and then rewritten it in garbled accord with Freud's: hence the confusion, and the effect of superimposition, which bothers Mr. Schorer and many other readers. But if this is so, then the novel takes its strength from

Lawrence's psychology and its weakness (inadvertently) from Freud's" (200–201).

Art or artifice, inspiration or formal control, unconscious or conscious composition, remain the poles of critical debate. In a more recent article on *Sons and Lovers,* E. P. Shrubb agonizes over the difficulty of distinguishing conscious from unconscious "intentions":

> Questions about a novelist's intentions are always otiose, if for no other reason than because what any mature adult knows about his own intentions, let alone anyone else's, is that he doesn't know much about them; but part of what I mean by saying these references are "no accident" is perhaps that there does seem to be something *un*conscious about them, that they do not give the impressions of being the product of an accidental or contingent intention, but rather the product of an interest or concern that Lawrence didn't make the book out of but rather made the book out of Lawrence. (111)

Shrubb assumes that a writer's unconscious enters the text only if he writes unconsciously. Shrubb finds evidence of unconscious writing in Lawrence's descriptions of places like the Bottoms and Hell Row. But a counter example illustrates the difficulty of deciding what is conscious. Using the same evidence, Dorothy Van Ghent finds that Lawrence's intensely "organic" descriptions are evidence of the novel's formal coherence and control: "The controlling idea is expressed in the various episodes—the narrative logic of the book. It is also expressed in imagery—the book's poetic logic. . . . He seeks the objective equivalent of feeling in the image" (7–8).

The debate about Freud's influence is shaped by the critics' assumptions about authorship. Believing that conscious control impairs art, Lawrence's partisans minimize the effect of Freud's ideas, while Lawrence's detractors emphasize this influence. Both positions assume that formal design is opposed to psychoanalytic meaning. Rather than attribute Paul's unconscious feelings for his mother to Lawrence's unconscious, however, it is possible to conclude that Lawrence consciously ascribed unconscious motives to Paul.

Freud provided exactly what editors said was missing—a thematic principle to unify disparate events. Begun as an autobiographical novel, *Sons and Lovers* was criticized for being too formless. Lawrence needed a way to transcend his personal material. Frieda Weekley,

John Worthen argues, deserves full credit for helping him "cut through the emotional tangles of the book which he had been trying to write his way out of for the previous two years" (*Idea* 42). Describing the draft she influenced in a letter to Garnett, Lawrence recognized that she helped him see the larger meaning of his story: "It's the tragedy of thousands of young men in England" (Boulton 1:477). Lawrence needed to see Paul's story as something more than autobiography. Freud's theories allowed him to see his experiences as typical rather than unique, illustrative rather than pathological. Only when he had nearly finished the final revision did he change the title from the specific "Paul Morel" to the general *Sons and Lovers* (*Idea* 38). For a writer schooled in the aesthetic importance of impersonality, this perspective was essential. With Garnett's assistance, in November Lawrence sent Duckworth his fourth complete revision of a manuscript that incorporated advice from his friends, two editors, and Frieda Weekley. *Sons and Lovers* owed its success to this process of criticism, extensive rewriting, and conscious formal control.

Depending on his writing for his livelihood, Lawrence was also concerned with sales. As a result, the characteristic modernist conflict between money and art erupted. Permitting Duckworth to make additional cuts for decency's sake, he justified revision as a financial necessity: "I don't mind if Duckworth crosses out a hundred shady pages in *Sons and Lovers*. It's got to sell, I've got to live" (Boulton 1:526). Yet believing art had an inviolable core, Lawrence could not write novels directly for the marketplace. He tried to distinguish commercial writing from art:

> I could do hack work, to a certain amount. But apply my creative self
> where it doesn't want to be applied, makes me feel I should bust or
> go cracked. I *couldn't* have done any more at that novel *[Sons and
> Lovers]*—at least for six months. I must go on producing, producing,
> and the stuff must come more and more to shape each year. But trim
> and garnish my stuff I cannot—it *must* go. (Boulton 1:501)

Lawrence regarded his "creative self" as a force beyond his control, but so was his practical self. Despite his claim that he could do "hack work" at will, he was unable to write without engaging his creative self. The genesis of "The Sisters," the forerunner of *The Rainbow*

(1915) and *Women in Love* (1920), illustrates his dilemma. Attempting to satisfy publishers' requests for another novel to capitalize on the success of *Sons and Lovers*, he promised that "The Sisters" would be shorter and "impeccable" (Boulton 1:526). But as he progressed, the material exceeded these bounds:

> I did 200 pages of a novel—a novel I love *[The Lost Girl]*—then I put it aside to do a pot-boiler ["The Sisters"]—it was too improper. The pot-boiler is at page 110, and has developed into an earnest and painful work—God help it and me. (Boulton 1:536)

Begun as a "pot-boiler" to meet publishers' specifications, "The Sisters" became an "earnest and painful work."

His intention was to proclaim a sexual gospel for the times:

> Pray to your Gods for me that *Sons and Lovers* shall succeed. People *should* begin to take me seriously now. And I do so break my heart over England, when I read the *New Machiavelli*. And I am so sure that only through a readjustment between men and women, and a making free and healthy of the sex, will she get out of her present atrophy. Oh Lord, and if I don't "subdue my art to a metaphysic", as somebody very beautifully said of Hardy, I do write because I want folk—English folk—to alter, and have more sense. (Boulton 1:544)

Lawrence's deepening engagement in his work was no longer due to a Romantic desire to express his inner self, or a therapeutic release of emotion as it had been in *The Trespasser,* but was the result of a strong and clear rhetorical purpose. Wanting a "readjustment between men and women" and a freeing "of the sex" in everyday life, he rejected any "metaphysic."

When Garnett pointed out formal problems in "The Sisters," Lawrence agreed that the character who became Ursula was "incoherent" and her first affair was "wrong" (Boulton 2:142), but he refused to alter his basic purpose. He wanted Garnett's approval yet felt confident enough to pursue his intention whatever Garnett thought. Lawrence had already tired of the *Sons and Lovers* kind of book:

> In a few days time I shall send you the first half of the Sisters—which I should rather call The Wedding Ring—to Duckworths. It is *very* different from *Sons and Lovers:* written in another language almost. I shall

be sorry if you don't like it, but am prepared.—I shan't write in the same manner as *Sons and Lovers* again, I think: in that hard, violent style full of sensation and presentation. You must see what you think of the new style. (Boulton 2:132)

Trying to reduce the autobiographical content and realism in his fiction, he adopted a new aesthetic.

To move beyond the personal, Lawrence attempted to articulate a collective vision. He wanted to be more than the sum of his subjective, personal experiences:

You see it really means something—I *wish* I could express myself— this feeling that one is not only a little individual living a little individual life, but that one is in oneself the whole of mankind, and ones [*sic*] fate is the fate of the whole of mankind, and ones charge is the charge of the whole of mankind. Not *me*—the little, vain, personal D. H. Lawrence—but that unnameable me which is not vain nor personal, but strong, and glad, and ultimately sure, but so blind, so groping, so tongue-tied, so staggering. (Boulton 2:302)

He conceived of a collective essence both intersubjective and communicable. Without resorting to generalization or abstraction, he wanted to find a constant in individual experience, or as he put it in his well-known metaphor, his subject was carbon whether in a diamond or a piece of coal. Although reached subjectively, this knowledge was impersonal, available to other people: "And art which is lyrical can now no longer satisfy us: each work of art that is true, now, must give expression to the great collective experience, not to the individual" (Boulton 2:301). Formal methods of achieving impersonality appealed to him for rhetorical reasons; they helped him identify what was constant and use it to reach his audience. Both as a professional author and as an artist with a social purpose, he wanted to overcome lyric subjectivity to establish a ground for communication with readers.

After the critical and commercial success of *Sons and Lovers*, the primary dispute between Lawrence and publishers was how "honest" he could be without risking prosecution. The sales of *Sons and Lovers* made Lawrence less receptive to publishers' formal criticism and censorship. His resistance was not a sign of new indifference to readers, but was instead a mark of increased confidence in his own judgment and his own value to publishers. With experience and critical recognition, Lawrence was in a position to argue with editors more forcefully. The main points of friction continued to be legal issues of obscenity and libel, which publishers could not afford to ignore. Always fully appreciating Lawrence's literary and commercial value, publishers tried to convince him to eliminate actionable passages, but their requests conflicted with his specific rhetorical goal—to jolt his readers into new lives. Despite this refusal to seek a public directly, his "creative self" sought a wide audience for his prophetic mission, as a 1914 letter to John Middleton Murry indicates:

> Don't give up feeling that people *do* want to hear what you say: or rather, they don't *want* to hear, but they need to, poor things. (Boulton 2:171)

"Hack work," trying to please an audience, was pandering, but changing it was a writer's duty. Lawrence's justification for seeking publication was that he had to transform his readers' lives.

In disputes with editors he insisted that his publishing experience had acquainted him with his proper audience and had taught him how to reach it. He wanted to be a messenger for his own generation: "I think, do you know, I have inside me a sort of answer to the *want* of today: to the real, deep want of the English people, not to just what they fancy they want. And gradually, I shall get my hold on them" (Boulton 1:511). As an artist he was obliged to address himself to present and future readers. They would vindicate him—and justify publishers' faith: "Tell Methuen, he need not be afraid. If the novel doesn't pay him back this year, it will before very long. Does he expect me to be popular? I shan't be that. But I am a safe speculation for a publisher" (Boulton 2:370). He also asked his publisher and editor to appreciate his goal before offering him advice: "You know how willing I am to hear what you have to say, and to take your advice and to act on it when I have taken it. But it is no good unless you will have patience and understand what I *want* to do" (Boulton 2:165).

Lawrence knew that violating contemporary moral standards was financially risky. Determined to be explicit where others were suggestive, he broke the code governing what could be implied but not stated. He felt his honesty was thoroughly moral, and he believed this justification would be sufficient for his publisher as well. He urged his first agent, J. B. Pinker, to enlist Methuen's support:

> Do you think Methuen is ready to back up this novel of mine? He must make some fight for it. It is worth it, and he must do it. It will never be popular. But he can make it known what it is, and prevent the mean little fry from pulling it down. Later, I think I must go and see him. There will be a bit of a fight before my novels are admitted, that I know. The fight will have to be made, that is all. The field is there to conquer. (Boulton 2:294)

Lawrence tried to reassure Pinker that *The Rainbow* would be acceptable: "Therefore tell Methuen if he asks . . . that there shall be no very flagrant love-passages in it (at least, to my thinking)" (Boulton 2:270). Although he promised Pinker he would cooperate with Methuen, Lawrence also warned he would not mutilate his book:

> I hope you are willing to fight for this novel. It is nearly three years of hard work, and I am proud of it, and it must be stood up for. I'm afraid there are parts of it Methuen wont [*sic*] want to publish. He must. I will take out sentences and phrases, but I won't take out paragraphs or pages. So you must tell me in detail if there are real objections to printing any parts. (Boulton 2:327)

Lawrence believed that his audience would emerge after the First World War. As much as he loathed the war and suffered from it, he correctly predicted that it would reform literary taste. He wrote Pinker:

> I am glad of this war. It kicks the pasteboard bottom in the usual "good" popular novel. People have felt much more deeply and strongly these last few months, and they are not going to let themselves be taken in by "serious" works whose feeling is shallower than that of the official army reports. (Boulton 2:240)

He argued that the trauma of war would make readers scorn superficial feeling in conventional fiction. Disillusionment would prepare them to respond to his fiction because it was free of prewar cant.

In periods of dejection, however, his dread of publishing returned. When he despaired of acclaim, he felt vulnerable to public opinion.

Although Lawrence knew what he wanted his readers to become, he did not really know who they were. Assessing the diverse twentieth century reading public, he echoed Flaubert's demand to be judged by his peers:

> I refuse to be judged by them. It is not for them to exculpate or to blame me. They are not my peers. Where are my peers? I acknowledge no more than five or six—not so many—in the world. But one must take care of the pack. . . . Be careful of them. (Boulton 2:352)

Lingering over *The Rainbow,* he wrote, "What is the use of giving books to the swinish public in its present state" (Boulton 2:276). He confessed to Pinker, "For my own part, I always shrink from having my work published. I hate the public to read it" (Boulton 2:294). Finally sending Pinker the completed manuscript at the end of May 1915, Lawrence expressed his usual regret at releasing his work to scrutiny as well as his uncertainty about its propriety:

> I hope you will like the book: also that it is not very improper. It did not seem to me very improper, as I went through it. But then I feel very incompetent to judge on that point.
>
> My beloved book, I am sorry to give it to you to be printed. I could weep tears in my heart, when I read these pages. If I had my way, I would put off the publishing yet a while. (Boulton 2:349)

Despite Lawrence's characteristic ambivalence about publishing, the demand for his fiction was increasing. In October, an American agent wrote Pinker that Alfred Knopf was interested in Lawrence and expected him "to ultimately make very good in a big way" (Pinker Papers, 21 October 1915).

Although Lawrence frequently protested that he had done nothing illegal or immoral, he fully intended to violate legal and moral codes. Like other modernists, Lawrence based his rhetorical stance on opposition to contemporary society. He felt blind rage: "For I am hostile, hostile, hostile to all that is, in our public and national life. I want to destroy it" (Boulton 2:328). Attacking a society already besieged by war, he met immediate censorship. Despite the early support of publishers, critics, and readers, Lawrence's work became unpublishable because it was illegal. In November 1915, *The Rainbow* was declared obscene, and Methuen was ordered to destroy all copies. The immediate result was that the price rose sharply:

> That was a ridiculous affair, instigated by the National Purity League, Dr Horton and Co, nonconformity. Of course I achieved a good deal of notoriety, if not fame, am become one of the regular topics. But the whole thing is nasty and offensive.—I heard that Hatchard's had sold their last copy of the *Rainbow,* sub rosa, for four guineas. (Boulton 2:477)

Lawrence's agent believed the prosecution could be fought. Frank Swinnerton urged Pinker to support Lawrence: "I can't help thinking it *is* rather gross; but I still believe that Lawrence's power and intensity are without parallel or rival among the younger writers, and I am extremely sorry about the whole squalid prosecution business" (Pinker Papers, 8 December 1915). Pinker testified before the Westminster Tribunal (Pinker Papers, 25 February 1916). According to Ezra Pound, Pinker blamed Methuen for caving in to a mere magistrate:

> [Pinker] put the whole blame on Methuen. Some crank went to a magistrate and said the book was immoral. Methuen admitted it. Then the magistrate gave various orders, *in excess of his powers.* If Methuen had declined to obey, or if they had denied that the book was immoral, NOTHING could have been done until the Home Office moved. The Home Office had inspected the book (Mr Birrell being asked for an opinion said the book was too dull to bother about) and decided that they would do nothing. (Read 283)

Mr. Birrell's opinion anticipates Judge Woolsey's ruling on *Ulysses:* a difficult or dull novel could not be obscene. At the time, however, Pound was correct in informing Joyce that publishers were wary of controversial fiction. Sales had guaranteed publishers' support for Lawrence until the war agitated government officials in unpredictable ways. Before the war, libraries had circulated *Sons and Lovers,* but after *The Rainbow* was suppressed, publishers themselves anticipated and enforced censors' objections to explicit sexual passages.

Lawrence tried to rally powerful friends to defend his book, but nothing could be done in wartime. Amy Lowell frankly proposed a compromise to make his work publishable, but he refused on the grounds that any tampering would destroy what was distinctive:

> No, Amy, again you are not right when you say the india-rubber eraser would let me through into a paradise of popularity. Without the india-rubber I am damned along with the evil, with the india-rubber

> I am damned among the disappointing. You see what it is to have a
> reputation. (Boulton 3:296)

His reply illustrates how ideology framed his choices. Pretending to
be contemptuous of the "paradise of popularity," Lawrence claims
that the public will consider him either evil or disappointing, erotic
or boring, and he rejects each characterization. He implies that "popularity" requires him to sacrifice his originality. But publishers' sustained interest in his work indicates that literary popularity was not
at issue. Once revision was demanded by censors rather than editors,
compliance became an ethical and political compromise. To change
his work in response to a threat would be moral cowardice.

As wartime hysteria deprived Lawrence of any opportunity to
reach an audience, he periodically retreated to Romantic aesthetics.
Discussing this period, Worthen also notes Lawrence's contradictory
statements: "In such contradictions, we can understand Lawrence. . . .
He might feel unutterably alienated, but he could still express that
desire to affect people, to alter the course of their lives" (*Idea* 86).
Feeling that *Women in Love* progressed rapidly because it was the
book of his "free soul" (Boulton 2:614), he claimed he wrote it without regard for the immediate public:

> The world will go its own way, and I shall go mine: if only it will let
> me alone. What I write now I write for the gods. I am useless to this
> mankind, and this mankind is useless to me. It is no good pretend-
> ing any more that there is a relation between it and me. If only it will
> let me alone, and not try to destroy my own inner world, which is
> real, I don't mind. But my life is not any more of this world, this
> world of this humanity, and I won't pretend it is. (Boulton 2:580)

Contempt for the public reinforced his isolation:

> But already it is beyond all hope of ever being published, because of
> the things it says. And more than that, it is beyond all possibility even
> to offer it to a world, a putrescent mankind like ours. I feel I cannot
> *touch* humanity, even in thought, it is abhorrent to me.
>   But a work of art is an act of faith, as Michael Angelo says, and
> one goes on writing, to the unseen witnesses. (Boulton 2:602)

Nor could he write for money:

> What is more, I can't write stories to make money, because I don't
> want to. Curse the idiotic editors and the more idiotic people who

read: shall I pander to their maudlin taste. They bore me. (Boulton 2:587)

These expressions of indifference to his audience were as strong as any postmodernist's. Although this attitude prevailed after the war, it was still intermittent while he was writing *Women in Love.*

Contemporary with these outpourings of rhetorical despair were assertions that he would win a public soon. He continued to borrow money from his literary agent by rationalizing that Pinker would profit later (Boulton 2:629). Pinker lent the money because he also believed in Lawrence's future, and Lawrence thanked him for his confidence (Boulton 2:630). Lawrence promised Pinker that after his novel was finished, he would *"only* write stories *to sell"* (Boulton 2:637). Publishers continued to express interest in Lawrence's work. He told Pinker in April 1917: "Eveleigh Nash says he would like to see *Women in Love.* Somehow I don't want it published, even if it were possible, just yet" (Boulton 3:111). In November, Fisher Unwin also inquired about the novel (Boulton 3:184).

Even this deliberately impersonal book filled him with dread at releasing it to public scrutiny:

> As for my novel, I don't know if I hate it or not. I think everybody else will hate it. But this cannot be helped. I know it is true, the book. And it is another world, in which I can live apart from this foul world which I will not accept or acknowledge or even enter. The world of my novel is big and fearless—yes, I love it, and love it passionately. It only seems to me horrible to have to publish it. (Boulton 2:659)

This self-protective attitude cannot have pleased his agent or publishers. Lawrence directed his frustration at his agent, and he left Pinker for the Curtis Brown agency in 1921. He wrote a friend:

> I wrote and told Pinker I must soon have more money. He does not answer. Probably he does not want to advance any more. Tant pis pour lui—I am just as well satisfied. My relations with that little parvenu snob of a procureur of books were always strained, best have them broken. (Boulton 3:136)

If Pinker was a "parvenu snob," what was Lawrence? Projecting aspects of his own social uneasiness onto Pinker, he focused on the secondary mediator between his work and the public. Lawrence used the metaphor of prostitution to convey the division he felt between the process of producing his art and the need to sell it. Associating money with anything of spiritual value made him feel that he was corrupting the purity of the work. Although only the threat of prosecution checked publishers' enthusiasm, Lawrence turned against them. Publishers were easy targets because they were intermediaries between writers and readers. They judged manuscripts, and they handled the money.

Driven to contradiction, Lawrence argued that *Women in Love* was safer than *The Rainbow:* "But again, I don't think this book is likely to be suppressed for *immorality,* like the *Rainbow,* God knows how it will go" (Boulton 3:29). Yet a contemporary letter to a friend expressed his usual doubts before publication:

> Today I have sent off the MS. of my new novel *Women in Love.* Can I tell you how thankful I am to have the thing done, and out of the house!—But I have a great respect for this new book. I think it is a great book—though no doubt I shall share the opinion with nobody.—Whether the book will ever get published, I do not know—and don't greatly care. It seems such a desecration of oneself to give it to the extant world. (Boulton 3:35)

Despite publishers' support, he was again uncertain about the new novel's reception, defensive about its value, and embarrassed by his vulnerability.

Commercial publishers felt he had abandoned them, not the reverse. They recognized the economic value of Lawrence's eroticism yet could not violate legal standards. As early as 1919, they were competing to buy manuscripts they could not openly publish. Martin Secker wanted to release *Women in Love* under its old title, "The Sisters" (Boulton 3:391), but negotiations broke down when Lawrence insisted that *The Rainbow* had to be included in the agreement. Secker offered £200 for all rights to *The Rainbow,* but Lawrence declined these terms in favor of Duckworth's willingness to offer royalties. Secker refused to match Duckworth's offer, arguing that Lawrence's books were unprofitable. Nevertheless, he was willing to offer substantial sums—£300 for *Women in Love* and £200 for *The Rainbow*—if Lawrence would relinquish royalties. Secker told an intermediary: "But I am a little tired of the whole thing and, now Duckworth is in competition, am quite ready to retire in his favour.

Lawrence's books are not worth competing for from a money making point of view" (Boulton 3:460, n1). Secker's offers indicate that he was weighing risk against potential profit. The risk was worth taking for a high rate of return but not for shared gains. Meanwhile, Duckworth withdrew his offer when Lawrence refused to delete a potentially actionable chapter from *The Rainbow*. Lawrence frankly told Secker what had happened and asked to reopen negotiations. This time Secker agreed to royalties and a £100 advance on both *The Rainbow* and *Women in Love* (Boulton 3:499).

Explaining publishers' interests, B. W. Huebsch, who bought the American rights, affirmed the value of steady sales:

> The degree of my interest is not to be measured by the extent of the sales, but I think that my methods will probably be advantageous to you in the long run even though the immediate results may seem rather meager. The demand for your books, though not large, is persistent. I much prefer this to the more rocket-like success. (Boulton 3:356, n1)

Although Huebsch was unable to publicize *The Rainbow* because he feared prosecution, he quietly sold out an edition:

> I withheld the book when the ghouls were lying in wait for me to publish it, and a few months ago I quietly distributed the edition that I had prepared in the autumn of 1915 without advertising or any other publicity, so that at least the book is not buried. (Boulton 3:356, n1)

As news of *The Rainbow* prosecution spread, the demand for copies increased. Lawrence saw that privately distributed books could be profitable (Boulton 2:449, 462). He did not exploit this phenomenon successfully until he wrote *Lady Chatterley's Lover,* but he saw its possibilities at once. In collaboration with John Middleton Murry and Philip Heseltine, he developed a proposal for authors to publish their own books. They had two main goals: to rescue worthwhile manuscripts rejected by other publishers and to bring this work to the public's attention.

The cooperative venture appealed to Lawrence's lifelong desire for a community of like-thinking people, but his own publishing experiences did not support the first part of its rationale. He knew

Sons and Lovers had not earned its advance, yet Duckworth offered to publish *The Rainbow* on the same terms (which Lawrence rejected as paltry), and Methuen tripled this offer. Both publishers recognized the quality of Lawrence's writing and were willing to invest their money to support their literary judgment. In contrast, seven hundred copies of the cooperative venture's advertising circular produced only thirty replies (Boulton 2:605).

Lawrence's second point had more justification. As the number of books increased, the best were easily overlooked in the deluge of titles. Private publishing was a way to certify work Lawrence and his partners approved. Private publishing would also overcome both of his objections to commercial firms—the taint of money and the need to conform to the public's standards of decency:

> I think there ought to be some system of private publication and private circulation. I disbelieve *utterly* in the public, in humanity, in the mass. There should be again a body of esoteric doctrine, defended from the herd. The herd will destroy everything. (Boulton 3:143)

His hope that private publishing would preserve the purity of his vision from editorial compromise and commercialism proved fruitless at this time, but it flourished after the war when private presses emerged to fill the gap between conventional morality and avant-garde taste (Ford 352).

Although it was not lack of a publisher that had stifled *The Rainbow*, the underground aspect of private publishing also appealed to Lawrence. He liked to think of himself as an outlaw: "I feel quite anti-social, against this social whole as it exists. I wish one could be a pirate or a highwayman in these days" (Boulton 2:540). Lawrence encouraged Heseltine with the familiar cliché that they had to battle philistine oppression: "we will make the bombs to smite the Philistine. Oh to *bust* up the Philistine—only that" (Boulton 2:551).

Unable to reach a public in England, Lawrence summoned the energy to seek one elsewhere. So important was the social aspect of his fiction that in 1917 he tried to cultivate an audience in America rather than write only for himself. He knew little about the American market, but he believed that living in America would stimulate him. He told Pinker:

> It is necessary now for me to address a new public. You must see that. It is no use my writing in England for the English any more. . . . I hope you don't feel uneasy about my work. I tell you it is true and unlying, and will last out all the other stuff. It is really necessary for me now to move under a new sky—it is a violation to be shut up here any longer. (Boulton 3:73)

His idea of America was more important to him than the actual place, and he seems to have been reluctant to test the idea against reality. During the war he was not permitted to leave England, and when he could travel, he went not to America but to Italy.

Lawrence began to rely on the American firm of Thomas Seltzer: "Nowadays I depend almost entirely on America for my living" (Boulton 4:114). The turning point for Lawrence was Seltzer's willingness to fight censorship. In 1922 Seltzer won a "suppression" trial for *Women in Love* (Boulton 4:296). In a few months it sold fifteen thousand copies, a figure that puzzled Lawrence: "Why do they read me? But anyhow, they *do* read me—which is more than England does" (Boulton 4:363). His question begs for reassurance that the public's interest was not merely prurient. Seltzer provided the guarantee that whatever he wrote would be published, freeing Lawrence to follow an inner program: "I feel hopeless about the public. Not that I care about them. I want to live my life, and say my say, and the public can die its own death in its own way, just as it likes" (Boulton 4:111). In this mood, he could not believe those "poor things," his readers, needed his message.

The fiction Lawrence wrote after the war is widely regarded as a falling off, but explanations of the decline vary. It has been attributed to sheer exhaustion after writing three masterpieces as well as to frustration that he could not publish two of them (Ingersoll 309). Deliberately isolating himself in remote places, Lawrence lost not only his connection to readers, but his conviction that his work was urgent. Moving to Italy, he abandoned his audience: "I am not interested in the public—it all seems so far off, here in Sicily—like another world" (Boulton 3:486). Estranged from readers, Lawrence's attitude to his audience affected both the content and the narrative form of his fiction. He became more strident in expressing his convictions and more explicit in addressing the reader.

The narrative point of view in the fiction of the early 1920s suggests that Lawrence's uncertainty about his rhetorical relationship to his audience was also responsible for the new style. Worthen calls the appearance of the intrusive narrator Lawrence's "popular style," linking it to his pursuit of an audience (*Idea* 127). It seems popular, however, only if the narrator's direct address seems similar to nineteenth-century novelists' use of the form to establish intimacy.

In nineteenth-century novels, direct address is generally interpreted as a sign of familiarity between author and reader.[6] But postmodernism has given authorial intrusions another significance: they seem a recognition of the artificiality of all attempts at representation. Direct address has become a sign of distance from the reader, as the narrator attempts to invoke what is absent. Barbara Johnson's analysis of the effect of apostrophe in lyric poetry is also pertinent to novelists' conceptions of readers:

> Apostrophe in the sense in which I will be using it involves the direct address of an absent, dead, or inanimate being by a first-person speaker. . . . Apostrophe is a form of ventriloquism through which the speaker throws voice, life, and human form into the addressee, turning its silence into mute responsiveness. (185)

By stipulating a relationship between narrator and reader, apostrophe indicates that the relationship does not yet exist. Addressing a specific reader, apostrophe departs from the modernist aesthetic of impersonal art and its usual manifestation in free indirect discourse, but it anticipates the postmodernist's rhetorical stance.[7]

As Lawrence traveled farther from his audience, his narrators began to resemble the intrusive first-person narrators of postmodernist fiction who often express illicit desires and taboo beliefs. Rick Rylance attributes Lawrence's extreme positions in this period to his isolation: "The rightwards drift of Lawrence's thought is continuous with his increasing separation from his own social origins and experience" (167). Yet Rylance also points out that Lawrence's stance was essentially critical, dissenting from orthodoxy on both the left and the right. If his ideas about sex offended the right, his views on politics alienated the left. The full range of opinions his characters express is often ignored. Although critics usually attribute the views farthest to the right to Lawrence himself, these ideas are always qualified by characters, usually women, who dispute them and plots that undermine them.[8]

While trying to assure publication for *Women in Love* and *The Rainbow,* which he considered his best books (Boulton 3: 519), Lawrence resumed work on *The Lost Girl* abroad. Expanding a sketch called "Elsa Culverwell" as the kernel of his novel, Lawrence rejected the first-person narrator of the early draft (published in an appendix to the Cambridge edition). This point of view is as awkward in the story as it is in his first novel. When Elsa attempts to convey the wisdom of hindsight as well as the immediacy of present events, "she" achieves neither:

> I still was not very handsome: cold looking, with my slightly aquiline nose and my steady blue eyes. I had dun-colored hair, I was pale. But I had the knack of looking a lady. (356)

In *The Lost Girl* Lawrence replaced Elsa with Alvina Houghton and allowed himself to depart from his "intimate" style. His use of varied narrative styles, his inconsistent tone, his parodic allusions to a canonical model, and his mocking asides to the reader are all characteristics of postmodernist fiction. Set in a town named "Woodhouse," the novel explicitly signals its debt to *Emma.* Like Jane Austen, Lawrence examines how a young woman weighs social class and sexual desire as she chooses a husband. Unlike Emma, however, Alvina Houghton follows her desire.

Despising men of her own social milieu and dreading spinsterhood, Alvina marries Ciccio, an Italian peasant she meets when he is employed as a dancer in the Natcha-Kee-Tawara Company, an international troupe of young men led by a female star and impresario. As their name suggests, they perform imitations of Native American dances. The narrator exploits the comic potential of the itinerant performers, but he also shows how seriously Alvina is attracted to their way of life. They may be untrained dancers and fake Indians, but they offer an erotic and communal alternative to Woodhouse. Nevertheless, Alvina does not depart with them. Instead, she gets a job as a nurse, and the realistic social criticism of this section seems to belong in another novel.

At times, the narrator in *The Lost Girl* resembles the narrators of *The Rainbow* and *Women in Love*. In contrast to the comparable passage in "Elsa Culverwell," the omniscient perspective here infuses Alvina's appearance with ambiguity by describing hidden qualities as well as visible ones:

> She grew up a slim girl, rather distinguished in appearance, with a slender face, a fine, slightly arched nose, and beautiful grey-blue eyes over which the lids tilted with a very odd, sardonic tilt. The sardonic quality was, however, quite in abeyance. She was ladylike, not vehement at all. (21)

The omniscient perspective also makes it possible to emphasize certain events: "Afterwards, later on, when she was inclined to criticise him, she would remember the moment when she saw his face at the Italian Consulate in London" (290). Expressing how much Ciccio captivates Alvina as well as how short-lived the feeling will be, this comment compresses present and future perceptions. Finally, Lawrence uses the "intimate" style of his major work when Alvina journeys to Italy with Ciccio. This section, which Worthen compares to Lawrence's best work as "exploratory" (*Idea* 115), probes the unconscious feelings of Alvina and Ciccio:

> Then deliberately she got out of bed, and went across to him. He was horrible and frightening, but he was warm. She felt his power and his warmth invade her and extinguish her. The mad and desperate passion that was in him sent her completely unconscious again, completely unconscious. (313)

But Lawrence does not use his "intimate" style consistently. Transgressing the strictures of modernist form, the narrator's tone and style shift rapidly. The tone is ironic when he provides an account of James Houghton, Alvina's father:

> That Woodhouse, as a very condition of its own being, hated any approach to originality or real taste, this James Houghton could never learn. He thought he had not been clever enough, when he had been far, far too clever already. (5)

In contrast to Lawrence's three previous novels, here the narrator mocks characters he dislikes and refuses to plumb their unconscious motives. Whereas in *The Rainbow* and *Women in Love* the narrator examines Anton Skrebensky as well as Will Brangwen, Loerke as well as Birkin, in *The Lost Girl* he can only jeer at James Houghton. Rather than penetrate Houghton's vanity to uncover his unconscious motives, the narrator ridicules his pretensions. While omniscient, the narrator is not impersonal.

The intrusive narrator does penetrate Alvina's unconscious:

> She remained for twenty years the demure, refined creature of her governess' desire. But there was an odd, derisive look at the back of her eyes, a look of old knowledge and deliberate derision. She herself was unconscious of it. But it was there. And this it was, perhaps, that scared away the young men. (21)

Although he articulates feelings that Alvina is not conscious of having and offers an hypothesis to explain them, he differs from the narrators of the "intimate" style in expressing an opinion beyond hers in the last sentence.

While the narrator mocks respectability and glorifies desire, he also notes the cost of Alvina's decision to marry Ciccio. Lawrence submits the title to a series of glosses which make the theme ambiguous. When Alvina decides to live with the theatre company during its run in Woodhouse, the townspeople regard her as a "lost girl," but she considers herself saved from the emptiness of respectable spinsterhood. Miss Pinnegar laments, "You're a lost girl!" and Alvina responds, "I like being lost" (217).

The narrator's comments complicate this formula of simple inversion of values. Although her middle-class respectability is what makes her attractive to Ciccio, the narrator notes that she had *"come down* in marrying Ciccio. She had lost caste" (289). She marries him for his sensuality, but he values her social status. This tacit marriage bargain is canceled when they return to his village in Italy. Her harrowing trip to Ciccio's home and her isolation among Italian peasants constitute a cautionary tale that contradicts the narrator's earlier endorsement of her desire for Ciccio. Pregnant and lonely in a remote mountain village, Alvina herself feels lost: "There is no mistake about it, Alvina was a lost girl. She was cut off from everything she belonged to" (314). This narrative validation of a comment others have made about her redefines "lost": the narrator observes, "The soul itself needs its own mysterious nourishment. This nourishment lacking, nothing is well" (314). The narrator's contempt for propriety is more unequivocal than his celebration of defiance. Alvina is a "lost girl" whatever she does.

By the time *The Lost Girl* was finished, Lawrence also felt lost. He could no longer anticipate readers' reactions:

> I read ½ of *The Lost Girl* in type—wonder how she'll seem to other people. It's different from all my other work: not immediate, not intimate—except the last bit: all set across a distance. It just came like that. May seem dull to some people—I can't judge. (Boulton 3:549)

Lawrence attributed the book to creative spontaneity: "It just came like that." Nevertheless, Worthen takes Lawrence's compliance with publishers' requests for revisions to meet the libraries' requirements as evidence of his eagerness to please the public. Lawrence wanted the book published, but he believed he was writing for himself.

Worthen argues that since Lawrence wanted this book to be popular, he was less engaged in it than in his previous work: "Its easiness is obviously partly a result of being made deliberately popular: we should remember Lawrence's own sense that 'one withdraws awhile from battle'—*The Lost Girl* is not a book that sets out to challenge its readers much" (*Idea* 113–14). It is hard to measure how challenging a book is because readers vary, but any reader who attempts to find a consistent way to interpret *The Lost Girl* will face a challenge, as Worthen himself implies when he describes the varied style: "it is certainly not a style in which much can happen outside the range of the narrator's dominant, flippant rhetoric. The novel is limited to certain kinds of interest in human nature precisely because the rhetoric is itself so rich" (*Idea* 109). Worthen seems to interpret Lawrence's desire to "withdraw from battle" as a willingness to make his work easier. But Lawrence sought readers more assiduously in his previous books than in his expatriate fiction. Withdrawing from battle was Lawrence's way to write as he pleased.

The ideological dichotomy between art and money controls Worthen's argument. He believes that Lawrence wrote with less attention to form when he needed money than when he wrote to meet his own standard. Worthen correlates Lawrence's major work with careful revision and his lesser work with rapid composition. While I agree with this assessment, I would argue that careful composition was the result of Lawrence's initial concern for readers, and he became lax when he felt isolated. The novels that resemble postmodernist fiction were written with less attention to form because readers seemed remote.

While intermittently working on *Aaron's Rod*, in 1920 Lawrence returned to *Mr Noon*, which employs his most radical narrative stance. Lawrence intended it to be a "comic novel—rather amusing but rather scandalous" (Boulton 3:639), yet comedy alone does not account for the change in his technique. Instead of maintaining a third-person omniscient point of view, he introduces a first-person narrator who is more fully developed as an outspoken character than the other intrusive narrators of this period.[9] His self-referential comments on the story anticipate postmodernist techniques. Some reviewers described the tone as "interjectory" and "carping," finding a distinct "truculence in mood," but others found it "dryly humourous" and "flippant," appreciating the realism of the dialogue. The "irony is gay on the surface and bitter below" (Vasey xxxvi–xxxvii). Since this novel was first published in its complete form in 1984, its affinities with postmodernism were readily perceived.[10]

Reporting his progress on *Mr Noon*, Lawrence wrote Secker that he was still unable to gauge readers' responses: "I get much wicked joy out of it. Probably you and the world will detest it. But it is unique. Which, from a publisher's point of view, is I know a misfortune" (Boulton 3:646). Later he warned Secker about *Mr Noon II*: it "is funny, but a hair-raiser. First part innocent . . ." (Boulton 3:702). Secker, however, was prepared to publish Part I:

> It is certainly excellent, and I fully share your enthusiasm for it. It is quite clear from the last page that it is complete as it stands, and that the author intends it to be published in a book by itself. (Boulton 3:717n)

Despite Secker's initial support, the first part of *Mr Noon* was not published until 1934, when it appeared in *A Modern Lover*. Part I proved too short for a book, and Part II seemed like a different work. Since Part I was based on a boyhood friend's experience and Part II was an account of his own elopement, the character of Gilbert Noon changes drastically. The narrator's tone also shifts from bedroom farce to satire. The target of derision in Part I is the characters; the target in Part II is the audience.[11] The narrator abandons any effort to create the "self-contained artefact" characteristic of modernism (Ingersoll 309). Parodying nineteenth-century authorial intrusions, the narrator speaks directly to his "dear reader."

In Part I, the narrator maintains a self-conscious distance from the story of Gilbert Noon's seduction of Emmie Bostock and invites the reader to share his amusement. This part is framed as an exemplum on the regional custom of "spooning." Calling attention to the artificiality of the story, the narrator apologizes, "Mr Noon was a first-rate spoon—the rhyme is unfortunate, though in truth, to be a first-rate spoon a man must be something of a poet" (21). Immediately following this observation, the narrator provides a typical Lawrentian representation of seduction in his "intimate" style:

> With his mouth he softly moved back the hair from her brow, in slow, dreamy movements, most faintly touching her forehead with the red of his lips, hardly perceptible, and then drawing aside her hair with his firmer mouth, slowly, with a long movement. She thrilled delicately, softly tuning up, in the dim continuous, negligent caress. (21)

Intruding and withdrawing, the narrator is performing for the reader, calling attention to the variety of methods in his repertoire. Teasing the reader, the narrator first refuses to represent sensuality for the reader's delectation and then presents it, emphasizing his control over the reader's response to the text.

In Part II, the narrator loses his distance from the narrative as he recounts a story based on Lawrence's first weeks with Frieda Weekley. As the narrator moves away from the audience and closer to events in Lawrence's own life, his tone shifts from mockery to the kind of prophetic fury Lawrence usually edited out of published work. Never revised for publication, Part II exhibits the raw exhortation of Lawrence's letters and *Phoenix*. Like *The Lost Girl*, *Mr Noon* defends the value of allowing passion rather than caution to rule one's life, and the argument has obvious personal motives. But reading Lawrence's fiction to learn about his life misrepresents the rhetorical effect of his writing. It is his writing that makes readers want to know how he lived.

In contrast to the farcical plot of Part I, which mocks lovemaking, here the narrator mocks the reader's interest in the lovemaking. When Gilbert Noon and Johanna are about to go to bed, the narrator refuses to narrate:

> But for the moment, I insist on apostrophising desire, intense individual desire, in order to give my hero time. Oh thunder-god, who sends the white passion of pure, sensual desire upon us, breaking through the sultry rottenness of our old blood like jagged lightening, and switching us into a new dynamic reaction, hail! Oh thunder-god, god of the dangerous bolts—!—No, gentle reader, please don't interrupt, I am *not* going to open the door of Johanna's room, not until Mr Noon opens it himself. I've been caught that way before. I have opened the door for you, and the moment you gave your first squeal in rushed the private detective you had kept in the background. Thank you, gentle reader, you can open your own doors. (137)

Lawrence resembles postmodernists not only in mocking the device of the intrusive narrator but in exposing the reader's assumption that the narrator can be identified with the author. The narrator is named "Lawrence," a writer whose other books have been criticized for indecency (Ingersoll 308). But the differences between author and narrator are evident in comments like this: "I can see absolutely no sounder ground for a permanent marriage than Johanna's—three times in a quarter of an hour, and so *well*" (146). This opinion belongs to "Lawrence" the libertine narrator critics attack, not to D. H. Lawrence, the moralizing author, who opposed this view both in *The Rainbow* and *Women in Love*.

Lawrence's difficulty in conceiving of his audience is evident in the long apostrophes to a series of imagined readers. His primary task is to inscribe a reader suited to his tale. He attacks the reader as "detestable," a "sniffing mongrel bitch of a reader," who needs to learn that "sweet lovey-doveyness" is "only half the show" (205). He shifts his target audience from a socially ambitious woman who "would never call an umbrella a brolly, much less a gamp" (24) to a salacious voyeur and critic: "Ah, dear reader, you don't need me to tell you how to sip love with a spoon, to get the juice out of it. . . . A spoon isn't a spade, thank goodness. As for a plough—don't mention it" (20–21). He installs his own reader in place of the nineteenth-century's:

> So there you are, gentle reader. It isn't my fault if I can't give you an idyll of coos. It would be good deal easier for me too. . . . And so, gentle reader—! But why the devil should I always *gentle-reader* you. You've been *gentle reader* for this last two hundred years. Time you had a change. Time you became rampageous reader, ferocious reader, surly, rabid reader, hell-cat of a reader, a tartar, a termagant, a tanger.—And so, hell-cat of a reader, let me tell you, with a flea in your ear, that all the ring-dove sonata you'll get out of me you've got already, and for the rest you've got to hear the howl of tom-cats like myself and she-cats like yourself, going it tooth and nail. (204–5)

The narrator's hostility to the reader becomes explicit as he insists on his control:

> I'm not talking about *your* little messy feelings and licentiousnesses, either. I'm talking about desire. So don't interrupt. Am *I* writing this book, or are you? Let me tell you, even if, gentle reader, you happen to be a wonderful, chirping, gentle, soft-billed gosling of a critic, gentilissimo, *I* am writing this book, and it is *not* being chirped out by you. That is the mistake you make, gentle critic. You think I ought to write down what you chirpingly dictate to me. But you're wrong, you fluffy little thing. I'm writing this book myself, and nobody is chirping it out to me like a piece of dictation. (137)

Bristling at criticism, Lawrence allowed his anger to enter the manuscript. He refused to write what the audience wanted to read. Lawrence may have intended this book to be commercial when he started it, but as he progressed, he allowed self-expression to overtake rhetorical aims. This, not *Women in Love,* was a book of his "free soul."

Aaron's Rod was also intended to be "innocent" (Boulton 3:702):

> Mountsier [Lawrence's agent] read the first half and didn't like it: takes upon himself to lecture me about it. Says it will be unpopular. Can't help it. It is what I mean, for the moment. It isn't "improper" at all: only it never turns the other cheek, and spits on ecstasy. I like it, because it kicks against the pricks. (Boulton 4:57)

As in *Mr Noon,* an intrusive first-person narrator controls the novel, shifting his focus from Aaron Sisson to other characters.[12] As an artist, Aaron is subjected to a series of social demands that threaten his work. Drawing attention away from the characters, the narrator describes the difficulties he confronts in trying to translate unconscious feelings into discourse:

> In his own powerful but subconscious fashion Aaron realised this. He was a musician. And hence even his deepest *ideas* were not word-ideas, his very thoughts were not composed of words and ideal concepts. They too, his thoughts and his ideas, were dark and invisible, as electric vibrations are invisible no matter how many words they may purport. If I, as a word-user, must translate his deep conscious vibrations into finite words, that is my own business. I do but make a translation of the man. He would speak in music. I speak with words. (164)

The narrator justifies both the impersonal and intrusive points of view in Lawrence's fiction. Only an external narrator can articulate a subject's "subconscious," and only an intrusive narrator can explain his rhetorical intentions. The narrator is the "word-user" who must "translate" the unconscious into language readers can understand.

Anticipating objections from the reader, the narrator justifies his practice and challenges the "gentle reader" to refute him:

> Don't grumble at me then, gentle reader, and swear at me that this damned fellow wasn't half clever enough to think all these smart things, and realise all these fine-drawn-out subtleties. You are quite right, he wasn't, yet it all resolved itself in him as I say, and it is for you to prove that it didn't. (164)

Here the narrative conventions of modernist fiction are acknowledged and opposed. The narrator goes beyond the character's self-knowledge and refuses to limit himself to free indirect discourse.[13]

Aaron expresses the distance Lawrence felt between himself and his audience. When writing Sir William Franks, Aaron realizes that he is addressing himself: "Well, here was a letter for a poor old man to receive. But, in the dryness of his withered mind, Aaron got it out of himself. When a man writes a letter to himself, it is a pity to post it to somebody else. Perhaps the same is true of a book" (264). As Lawrence's need to write for himself was consciously opposed to popularity, so Aaron refuses to do what he must to become a "success." Yet he perceives the power, the "cultural capital" in Pierre Bourdieu's phrase, of refusing to seek success. Sir William is fascinated by Aaron because Aaron does not envy him: "Aaron found himself paying homage too to the old man who had made a fortune. But also, exacting a certain deference in return, from the old man who had made a fortune. Getting it too. On what grounds? Youth, maybe. But mostly, scorn for fortunes and fortune-making" (154). Worthen argues that Lawrence's refusal to make the changes Seltzer requested indicates his commitment to the book, whatever readers might think (*Idea* 120). As Worthen says, "It is a novel unashamed of its obstinacy, as well as a novel astringently insistent on saying its say . . ." (*Idea* 130).

From Italy, Lawrence and Frieda went to Australia and then to New Mexico. Increasing the distance between his own culture and his settings, he acquired an ironic perspective on himself, particularly in *Kangaroo*. The intrusive first-person narrator addresses the reader directly when the characters cannot sustain the pitch of irony and abstraction he seeks. In the chapter titled "Harriett and Lovatt at Sea in Marriage," for example, a cynical analysis of three types of marriages is launched from a distance far beyond Lovatt's consciousness in an elaborate, sustained metaphor of ships tossed in ocean currents:

> Then, as I say, the hymeneal bark either founders, or dashes on a rock, or more wisely gets out of the clash of meeting oceans and takes one tide or the other, where the flood has things all its own way. (170)

The narrator admits that he does not know how to describe the "good bark" *Harriett and Lovatt:*

> I have not made up my mind whether she was a ship, or a bark, or a schooner, technically speaking. Let us imagine her as any one of them. Or perhaps she was a clipper, or a frigate, or a brig. All I insist is that she was not a steam-boat with a funnel, as most vessels are nowadays, sailing because they are stoked. (171)

The rest of the chapter examines the conflict between Harriett and Lovatt in terms of each one's conscious will and unconscious desire, like Lawrence's "intimate" novels. Foregrounding the metaphor as metaphor, however, breaks the frame of narrative verisimilitude.

Lovatt attempts to think through the metaphor to understand the pull and repulsion he feels with Harriett, but the narrator regards this attempt with irony.[14] The narrator prevents the reader from construing the metaphor as an explanation of marriage; it is purely a figure.

Similarly, Lovatt's self-judgment is judged by a narrator who justifies excessive introspection as a response to aesthetic demands:

> Now a novel is supposed to be a mere record of emotion—adventures, flounderings in feelings. We insist that a novel is, or should be, also a thought-adventure, if it is to be anything at all complete.
>
> "I am a fool," thought Richard to himself, "to imagine that I can flounder in a sympathetic universe like a fly in the ointment."—We think of ourselves, we think of the ointment, but we do not consider the fly. It fell into the ointment, crying: "Ah, here is a pure and balmy element in which all is unalloyed goodness. . . ." Hence the fly in the ointment: embalmed in balm. And our repugnance. . . . He preached, and the record was taken down for this gramophone of a novel. (279–80)

As Richard feels more and more isolated, the narrator addresses the reader directly to defend the improbability of the character as an accurate transcript of reality. Yet the narrator also claims that he alters reality for the reader's sake:

> "It has nothing to do with me," said Richard to himself—I hope, dear reader, you like plenty of *conversation* in a novel: it makes it so much lighter and brisker. (282)

Aware that Richard's metaphysical speculation has occupied most of the novel, the narrator defies the reader to complain. Offering a sarcastic apology, the narrator insists he has tried to make the novel "lighter and brisker" by rendering Richard's introspection as dialogue as much as possible.

After reaching a dead-end in both the rightist cult of personality and the leftist promises of socialism in *Kangaroo*, Lawrence tried to imagine a community worthy of commitment in *The Plumed Serpent*. Although its narrative form is similar to that of Lawrence's modernist fiction, this novel exceeds any modernist level of extremity. It has a realistic and a mythic plot. The former follows Kate Leslie, an Irish woman traveling in Mexico, as she observes factional battles for control of the revolution against Catholic and colonial institutions. She becomes friendly with Don Ramon and his family, who are landowners of European descent. As the leader of a faction that advocates spiritual regeneration through the native gods of Quetzalcoatl, Ramon introduces the novel's mythic plot, an escape from Western self-consciousness and apathy through ritual.

Kate's dilemma is that when she seeks autonomy, she finds alienation; when she identifies with a group, she overcomes alienation but sacrifices autonomy. She is drawn to Cipriano, a general in Ramon's army, erotically and politically because he allows her to feel a vicarious community with a group of Mexican peasants. Kate is a middle-aged woman whose European independence makes her attractive to Cipriano, yet she is also the kind of woman who equates being desired with feeling desire. Like Alvina and Ciccio in *The Lost Girl,* Kate wants sexual fulfillment while Cipriano wants social and political advancement.

The opposition between seeking fusion with another and fearing it is played out in sexual encounters between Kate and Cipriano as well as in domestic struggles between Ramon and his wife and in political battles between rival leaders. The couple, the family, and the state are parallel sites of contention. While showing the failure of the individual to find fulfillment alone (the European model), Lawrence also shows the difficulty of yielding individual identity to a group (Ramon's model). Lawrence presents the cult of Quetzalcoatl as a way to rescue the modern subject from the isolation of individualism, but he also expresses a bedrock of resistance against any emotion that obliterates self-consciousness.

The climax occurs when Ramon is installed as the "Living Quetzalcoatl" and orders the execution of three men. Combining idolatry and human sacrifice, this scene enacts what Conrad elides in "Heart of Darkness." Like Conrad, Lawrence tries to represent the unsayable through the unspeakable. In a despoiled church, Ramon's followers are "naked save for the black loincloths and the paint, and the scarlet feathers of the head-dresses" as they gather to the "hard drums of Huitzilopochtli" which are "beating incessantly outside, with a noise like madness" (381). As Ramon's disciple, Cipriano assumes the role of the "Living Huitzilopochtli," but the narrator continues to regard him as Cipriano:

Cipriano took a bright, thin dagger.

"The Lords of Life are Masters of Death," he said in a loud, clear voice.

And swift as lightning he stabbed the blindfolded men to the heart, with three swift, heavy stabs. Then he lifted the red dagger and threw it down. (380)

While Kurtz is the European who succumbs to inner savagery, Ramon is the descendant of Spanish colonists who institutes native sacrifice for communal regeneration. Lawrence seems to endorse what Conrad abhors. In contrast to Conrad's modernist use of myth as a transhistorical principle, Lawrence turns to indigenous myth as a functioning source of belief in peasant communities. He uses myth as a collective expression of desire which mediates between the individual and the community.

Although Lawrence's choice of peasants and non-English characters to represent the primitive quality of loss of consciousness is often interpreted as denigration of these groups, he idealized and envied this state.[15] In *The Plumed Serpent,* both Kate and the members of the cult find a connection between erotic pleasure and violence in the experience of losing self-consciousness. Before Kate is attracted to the cult, she is attracted to Cipriano because she imagines that he demands sexual submission: "Ah! and what a mystery of prone submission, on her part this huge erection would imply! Submission absolute, like the earth under the sky. Beneath an overarching absolute. . . . Language had abandoned her. . . . Her self had abandoned her . . ." (311–12). But this glorification of submission is only one pole of Kate's response. She immediately glosses her transport with a literary allusion: "My demon lover!" (312). Ecstasy beyond language seems to obliterate her sense of self, but the next moment she cites Coleridge. Her cultural identity persistently opposes her fantasy of submission. This oscillation between individuation and connection is never resolved. She continues to weigh independence against desire:

"Without Cipriano to touch me and limit me and submerge my will, I shall become a horrible, elderly female. I ought to *want* to be limited. I ought to be *glad* if a man will limit me with a strong will and a warm touch. . . . Rather than become elderly and a bit grisly, I will make my submission; as far as I need, and no further." (439)

This is not submission but a careful calculation of her options. She marries Cipriano in a civil ceremony, fully intending to return to Ireland a month later (421). She chooses to feign sexual submission rather than accept the only alternative she sees—no sexuality at all.

Kate begins where the reader does—appalled at the demanding rituals of Quetzalcoatl. As Kate gradually acknowledges the attraction of the cult, she prepares the reader to feel its appeal. Deflecting the reader's disgust at Huitzilopochtli's Night, Lawrence filters the ceremony through Kate's feelings:

> And deep in her soul came a revulsion against this manifestation of pure will. It was fascinating also. . . .
>
> At the same time, as is so often the case with any spell, it did not bind her completely. She was spell-bound, but not utterly acquiescent. In one corner of her soul was revulsion and a touch of nausea. (387)

Kate's initial opposition and gradual immersion in the communal mysticism of Ramon's cult provide a model for the reader. The obvious rhetorical intention is that as Kate expresses the reader's objections, her increasing fascination will draw the reader's approval with it. Nevertheless, her rational objections and her physical nausea never entirely disappear. As L. D. Clark notes, the text "incorporates, and reconciles within its form, the possibility of ironic reversal . . ." (84). Both Ramon's fantasy of spiritual regeneration through ritual murder and Kate's fantasy of erotic submission as an escape from isolation are contested by more realistic scenes of violence and revulsion.

Since Kate feels both the awe and the disgust extreme acts can elicit, a subversive, postmodernist reading of the novel is possible. The omniscient narrator's ability to penetrate Kate's unconscious as well as Ramon's and Cipriano's is essential to produce a double reading. At times, the narrator's observations merge with those of each character. In the passage above, for example, the clause "as is so often the case with any spell" seems to be a narrative generalization, but since it is embedded in the analysis of Kate's reactions, it may be her comment. Similarly, as Kate is watching a ceremony, the reader is told, "Oh, if there is one thing men need to learn, but the Mexican Indians especially, it is to collect each man his own soul together deep inside him, and to abide by it" (276). Is this Kate's opinion or the narrator's? Is Ramon's institution of ritual murder to be interpreted as a symbol or as a model for social action? Is Kate's submission to Cipriano a symptom of her malaise or a prescription for erotic fulfillment? Fearing that Lawrence intended the latter, many readers find this book repellent.

Most critics denounce *The Plumed Serpent* for its politics and pass over it as quickly as possible. Clark admits, "The weight of critical opinion has always been heavily against it" (8). Moore tries to apologize for it by arguing that Lawrence's "deeper self had been unable to believe, toward the last, in what he was writing" (*Intelligent Heart* 335). Although the book's prophetic purpose is clear, Clark tries to defend it by dismissing its political content and emphasizing its aesthetic form. He objects that the book's critics belong "to that numerous company who persist in ignoring Lawrence the artist and overstressing Lawrence the thinker" (9). Comparing the final text with the first draft, Clark focuses on its form, arguing that Lawrence's decision to develop Kate as a strong character and as the narrative's center of consciousness provides its unity (100).

Yet Graham Hough believes Lawrence was working "with what was perhaps the central revelation of his life," and "the transition from reporting to prophecy, whatever the quality of the prophecy, is no longer an uneasy switch—it is a real progress, accountable and accounted for within the narrative framework" (Hough 122). Tony Pinkney also defends this novel as the "most shrewd of modernist texts" (161), concluding that by the end of his career Lawrence was a "meta-modernist" (3). Pinkney mentions the use of an unreliable narrator and a "mythic method" as aspects of the novel's critique of modernism (154–58).[16]

However profound Lawrence's vision, his rhetorical stance was defiant. In this book Lawrence concedes less to the values he knew his audience held than in any other novel he wrote, including *Lady Chatterley's Lover*. Redemptive murder is far more repugnant than redemptive fornication. Lawrence stages violence in both mythic ritual and political action. By demonstrating the similarity between ritual and historical violence, he undercuts justifications of both. If murder enacts timeless mythic desires, it loses its political meaning. If it serves political factions, it loses its mythic resonance.

Like postmodernists, Lawrence addressed a society incapable of affirming any belief. Worthen notes how much Lawrence's postwar estrangement from readers affected this novel:

> *The Plumed Serpent* shows the chasm—which had been growing in his novels for years—between the artist whose idea of community was vital to him, whose idea of his novels was that they could change people—and the artist whose ultimate belief in any community he actually knew was nil, and whose novels had been in danger of turning into the monologues of a man alone in a wilderness of his own seeking. (*Idea* 166)

In *The Plumed Serpent,* Lawrence explores the benefits and dangers of a spiritual community as if he were talking to himself: as Kate feels listening to Ramon, "This was how Salome had looked at John" (182). From a modernist perspective, the scenes of violence and erotic domination seem to be Lawrence's way of incorporating myth into contemporary life. In a postmodern context, however, the offensive scenes in the novel acquire the force of a critique.

Anticipating a hostile response, Lawrence reaffirmed his commitment to *The Plumed Serpent* in his letters: "nobody will like it, but I think it's my most important" (Boulton 5:323). He wrote his American publisher, "I still think it is my most important novel: never mind the weary public. It too has got to grow up. But my 'Quetzalcoatl' novel will stand a lot of wear" (Boulton 5:320). Nevertheless, the public's failure to appreciate it upset him: "I could weep over *that* book, I do so hate it's [*sic*] being published and going into the tuppenny hands of the tuppenny public. Small private editions are really *much* more to my taste" (Boulton 5:387). Private publishing offered a way to reach sympathetic readers without submitting to public judgment.

Lawrence's restless period of self-imposed exile ended when he began *Lady Chatterley's Lover* in 1926 after a trip to England. In the course of writing the novel, he revived earlier plans for private publication. Norman Douglas showed Lawrence that this method could be successful and encouraged him to publish *Lady Chatterley* privately (Britton 213):

> I'm thinking I shall publish my novel *Lady Chatterley's Lover* here in Florence, myself, privately—as Douglas does—700 copies at 2

guineas. It is so "improper", it could never appear in the ordinary way—and I won't cut it about. So I want to do it myself—and perhaps make £600 or £700. (Boulton 6:225)

Private publishing allowed Lawrence to establish an intimate connection with a select group of readers and still earn money from his writing. Thanks to the publicity censorship provided, he could make more money by printing illegal manuscripts privately than by cooperating with commercial publishers.

Lawrence thought of his project partly as a mission to reform publishing: "I hate middle-men, and want to eliminate them as far as possible. If I can carry this thing through, it will be a start for all of us unpopular authors. Never let it be said I was a Bennett" (Boulton 6:343). Curtis Brown, his current agent, was one of the middlemen who would not share in the profits of private publication. He warned Lawrence not to destroy his "at last respectable reputation" (Boulton 6:353). Lawrence dismissed his agent's irritation: "Curtis Browns seem very huffed with me for making money on the private editions, apart from them. But they had such a scare over *Lady C.* how can they possibly handle the stuff I do in private" (Boulton 7:518). Knopf and Secker also encouraged him to revise the manuscript so they could publish it, but Lawrence hoped to earn more and compromise less by publishing privately. Another incentive to go underground was that new income tax regulations imposed a 20 percent deduction on royalties (Britton 231). Despite Lawrence's enthusiasm, Derek Britton apologizes for Lawrence's financial arrangements, illustrating the effect of the ideological conflict between art and money on critics:

> The desires to preserve his own and the novel's artistic integrity and to "take in the badly-needed shekels" . . . were of more or less equal status. Mercenary as the latter motive was, and at odds with the novel's teachings against money-lust, which are given greater prominence in the final version, it seems unreasonable to find fault with Lawrence in this; though it must also be acknowledged that in the importance he attached to the money-making aspect of private publication he fell short of his own high-minded principles. (242)

Censoring his novel to meet publishers' standards of decency might have been a sign of "money-lust," but the income *Lady Chatterley* provided was untainted by compromise. The highest of Lawrence's principles was to reach an audience, and the unprecedented sales figures for this novel suggest that he succeeded.

Independence from commercial publishers made *Lady Chatterley's Lover* possible. Confident that his manuscript would be published as written, Lawrence kept readers in mind as he revised. Private publication allowed Lawrence to feel closer to his readers than he had since leaving England after finishing *Women in Love*. Worthen believes "the mode of its production was a final and decisive influence on the kind of novel it became" (*Idea* 175). It became more public:

> Frieda Lawrence summed up the development by suggesting that the first version "he wrote as she came out of him, out of his own immediate self. In the third version he was also aware of his contemporaries' minds." . . . Such a distinction very properly stresses the public quality of the third version. (*Idea* 178)

Nevertheless, Worthen concludes that Lawrence "no longer had any sense of that relationship with his audience which had sustained even the loneliest of his previous novels" (*Idea* 182).

Similarly, Britton argues that Lawrence's memories of England rather than his connection to readers shaped the text. For Britton, the value of the novel is in its autobiographical sources, "in the throes of the painstaking and spiritually draining process of revising the first draft and investing the novel with a depth of feeling that had to be dredged up from the inner self" (Britton 184). Britton's judgment demonstrates the durability of the Romantic and psychoanalytic models of creativity. He argues that Lawrence's trip to England "provided him with fresh emotional and imaginative responses" that provided the setting for *Lady Chatterley* (Britton 117). The final draft expresses Lawrence's "desire to avenge himself while he still had life and strength to do so" (225):

> The bout of haemorrhages that preceded the writing of the final version was unquestionably the determining factor in the shift of outlook towards an unqualified, despairing revulsion for modern man and his works that was without precedent in any previous writings. The intrusive self, the raging misanthropy and the tendency to overstatement that distinguish *Lady Chatterley's Lover* emerge clearly from a

comparison of the responses to the awful singing of the Tevershall schoolchildren. (126)

While the qualities Britton mentions—the intrusive self, the raging misanthropy, the tendency to overstatement—would indicate that Lawrence was still writing for himself, they are far stronger in *Mr Noon* and other novels of the 1920s than in the final version of *Lady Chatterley's Lover*. Britton sees a "return to realism and the absence of authorial interpretation and didactic commentary" in the first draft but not in the final version (Britton 182). Conceding that revision was Lawrence's usual habit, Britton nevertheless argues that in this case the results were "detrimental" because Lawrence replaced "tenderness" with hostility to the middle and upper classes. The ideology of the spontaneous, expressive artist predisposes Britton to prefer the "more emotional" earlier drafts, but Lawrence decided their Blakean "lyricism and mysticism" were not fit for the public (Britton 249). Britton prefers the version that seems to express Lawrence's feelings rather than his conscious shaping of his material.

As he revised, Lawrence's rhetorical intention became more focused. The three versions of the novel show Lawrence's increasing control of form and structure, as well as his increasing commitment to readers. The narrator's tacit relation to the reader suggests that Lawrence felt so close to his audience that he did not need to invoke the reader's presence through apostrophe. Confidence in the novel's rhetorical effect allowed him to avoid the intrusive narrators of *Mr Noon, Aaron's Rod,* and *Kangaroo.* For the most part, the novel employs the symbolic realism, narrative omniscience, and "intimate" style of *Women in Love* and *The Rainbow.*[17] Knowing that publication was certain, Lawrence kept his readers' needs in mind.

Although written with flagrant disregard for contemporary standards of propriety, *Lady Chatterley's Lover* was also one of Lawrence's most blatantly didactic books. He felt he modified his inner voice less than he had in any other work, yet his rhetorical purpose was stronger here than anywhere else. Knowing the book would be considered immoral, Lawrence defended it on moral grounds: "My new novel is three parts done, and is so *absolutely* improper, in words, and so really *good,* I hope, in spirit—that I don't know what's going to happen to it" (Boulton 5:638). He vehemently affirmed the purity of the book, yet he conceded that he wanted it to shock the public: "I want subtly, but tremendously, to kick the backsides of the ball-less" (Boulton 6:72). Although Lawrence offered an internal justification for violating conventional morality, his purpose was not to express private thoughts but to change society: "As for writing pariah literature, a man has to write what is in him, and what he *can* write: and better by far have genuine pariah literature than sentimentalities on a 'higher' level" (Boulton 7:226). The "pariah" did not write for himself.

Lawrence appreciated the ironies of the market for limited editions. Increasing the price could increase the demand: "But this shows you the insanity of the modern collector of books. And a good author can't even get his work printed. Makes me tired! I hate this expensive edition business" (Boulton 7:304).Lawrence could now afford to mock commercial publishers' timidity because he had finally found a more profitable alternative. He knew he had a viable public:

> —and there is a big public waiting to get anything which they think is not orthodox, does not come via the "good" publishers. There is the enormous "proper" public, of Heinemann or Gollancz. But I believe the "improper" public is almost as big, if not bigger, so long as they are fairly safe. . . . But then I am amazed to realise how huge, and how much more potent the "improper" public is. (Boulton 7:448)

Here Lawrence was truly prophetic. He saw that alternative publishing for an "improper" minority public could produce a good income, and he foresaw that larger publishers would want to capture this market too.

In fact, *Lady Chatterley* was Lawrence's most profitable book. It was published in June 1928, and by the end of August, gross receipts were £980 (Boulton 6:533). His chief problems were filling orders before customs inspectors seized the books and collecting money from people who falsely claimed they had not received their copies. Demand was so great that the book was pirated, forcing Lawrence to print a second edition cheaper than the pirated copies. To remedy this situation, Lawrence asked Secker to publish an expurgated version to secure copyright (Britton 261). In 1959 Grove Press won the right to publish the first legal unexpurgated edition. Echoing

Lawrence's justification, the judge declared that since the novel was written as art and sold as art, it was not obscene. The reasoning of both men obeyed the ideology that art and money were antithetical, though the public submitted a dissenting opinion: 3,225,000 copies were sold in the first eight months of legal publication.

The central irony of Lawrence's career was that being unpublishable made him profitable. Both his income and audience were greatest when he had a clear idea of his readers in mind, a general public for *Sons and Lovers* and a private audience for *Lady Chatterley's Lover*. Unfairly blaming publishers for government censorship, he found a way to circumvent editorial and commercial restraints. As a result, he felt he could communicate with his readers directly. Thanks to private publishing ventures, he earned more from limited deluxe editions and illegal printings than from more reticent books. His most acclaimed works were written when he believed his readers urgently needed his message; his sales were greatest when readers believed the books were illicit.

CHAPTER FIVE

Why Art Pays

The ideology that art and money are antithetical was a reaction to the expansion and diversification of the literate audience in the nineteenth century. I have focused on the ways this antithesis shaped Flaubert's concept of the artist because modernists tried to emulate his ideal. Regarding the demographic changes in the audience as a threat to elite culture, Flaubert tried to fuse the Romantic idealization of the artist with a redefined model of the writer as professional. Since the elite public was necessarily a minority, highbrow writers could not accept sales as an index of literary value. Flaubert's example taught these writers to invoke the privileges of the professional as a way to distance themselves from those who wrote for a wider audience. Like members of other professions, he claimed that only his peers could evaluate his work and that he pursued a higher good than money. To demean writers he considered inferior, he accused them of putting profit above aesthetic values. Contempt for money became a defining feature of the serious artist, yet earning money was essential to maintain one's professional status. The modernist solution to Flaubert's dilemma was to use complex forms that seemed inaccessible to many readers as a way to demonstrate indifference to money and devotion to art. Since it was also necessary to earn a living by writing, however, modernists cultivated patrons and readers by generating publicity in the popular press.

As this ideology transformed popularity into a sign of mediocrity, formal innovation and difficulty became crucial qualities of art. Conrad, Joyce, and Lawrence believed that fiction could change readers' lives, yet the need to distinguish themselves from bestselling authors made them reluctant to address a wide audience. They were unable to articulate a social function for their fiction compatible with their aesthetic principles. If they called their aim moral or political, they would be harking back to discredited Victorian values. If they said they wanted their work to be emotionally stimulating or cathartic, they would be denying the modernist commitment to formalism. If they even admitted that they wanted to reach many readers, they would seem to be pandering. All three authors spoke of the reader's urgent need for their work, but they could not easily name the nature of this need.

The steady expansion of the literate audience undermined any assumptions authors might have made about readers when literacy was limited to a relatively homogeneous group. Unable to maintain the intimate rhetorical stance of earlier novelists, modernists responded to the distance between themselves and their readers by making narrative point of view a prominent concern. Although Conrad stated that his rhetorical intention was to make readers "see," his fiction undermines his assertions of human solidarity. He introduced Marlow to bridge the gulf he perceived between author and reader. Joyce felt so alienated from readers that he made narrative distance his primary aesthetic preoccupation. The profusion of narrative styles in *Ulysses,* for example, illustrates both the flexibility of the genre—it is possible to say almost anything in almost any style—and the difficulty of deciding on any single technique. As his formal innovations made his fiction increasingly inaccessible, however, he sacrificed the audience that the ambitious scope of his work seems to demand. Lawrence used first-person, omniscient, and intrusive narrators as his perception of his audience changed throughout his career.

The absence of an assumed rapport between author and reader was a serious challenge to the modernist novel. However communal other arts may be, novels claim to connect the individual writer to the individual reader. The paradigm of fiction is that only two people are present and that the intimacy between them can surpass ordinary

relationships. Walter Benjamin believed that the novel takes its justification from this personal connection—which he wanted to see
eliminated (310).[1] Benjamin's disapproval was based on his conception of the audience, just as modernist authors' aesthetic decisions
were based on their conceptions of the reader. Benjamin and other
Frankfurt School critics advanced a Marxist argument that capitalism
had produced a mass audience and had destroyed authentic popular
culture. Yet conservative critics expressed comparable contempt for
the mass audience because it failed to appreciate high art.[2] Both
camps persistently characterized the wide range of readers who make
some books bestsellers as a mass audience, but this concept itself
depends on the ideological antithesis between art and money, an
ideology so pervasive that it unites critics on the left and right.

Despite the tendency to blame capitalism for commodifying art
and producing a mass audience, the market supported high art as well
as bestsellers. Henry James, hardly an apologist for capitalism, saw
many benefits in the expansion and diversification of the reading
public:

> It is assuredly true that literature for the billion will not be literature
> as we have hitherto known it at its best. But if the billion give the
> pitch of production and circulation, they do something else besides;
> they hang before us a wide picture of opportunities—opportunities
> that would be opportunities still even if, reduced to the *minimum,*
> they should be only those offered by the vastness of the implied habi-
> tat and the complexity of the implied history. (653)

For the most part, critics on both the left and the right would accept
the truth of the first sentence but dispute the rest of James's analysis.
In contrast to those who vilify the mass audience, James realized that
the "public we somewhat loosely talk of as for literature or for anything else is really as subdivided as a chess-board, with each little
square confessing only to its own *kind* of accessibility" (653). Shifting
metaphors, he anticipated that "we may get individual publics posi-
tively more sifted and evolved than anywhere else, shoals of fish rising to more delicate bait" (654). James's account is an accurate
description of the actual market for modernism on both sides of the
Atlantic.[3] Books do not become bestsellers by appealing to a hypothetical common reader; high sales mean that a book appeals to many

segments of the public, and not necessarily for the same reasons. Thus, while modernist fiction initially attracted elite readers, it soon developed a wider audience and proved profitable.

Although the fragmentation of the audience presented a dilemma for authors, a market for a wide range of fiction stimulated the book trade. Publishers supplied the public with a proliferation of titles, including those that now constitute the modernist canon. Compensating for the distance between author and reader, publishers provided editors to mediate between the individual writer and the writer's likely audience. If writers could not know their public, at least they could know their editor. Editorial suggestions were sometimes heeded, sometimes ignored. But in either case, they provided early feedback for highbrow authors who felt isolated from other readers early in their careers and when their work failed to receive the attention they sought. As their confidence grew, they became more independent. Editors' advice has been maligned for serving commercial rather than literary interests, but editorial comments on modernist texts usually anticipated the subsequent critical consensus. Editors were committed to improving literary quality because they understood the economic advantages of the steady seller as well as the bestseller. Editors thought of themselves as midwives to literature rather than hucksters, and even publishers did not think of themselves as ordinary businessmen.

Demonstrating that commercial publishing institutions benefited literature, my argument differs from critiques that blame capitalism for failing to support art. Whether launched from a Marxist or an elitist perspective, however, objections to capitalism depend on the ideological dichotomy of inspiration and income. Two accounts of modernist publishing at odds with my own serve to illustrate the continuing influence of this dichotomy. Addressing many of the issues I raise, Russell A. Berman formulates an analysis influenced by the Frankfurt School. In contrast, Siegfried Unseld, former head of the German firm Suhrkamp Verlag, expresses the position of many commercial publishers of highbrow fiction. Although one is a detailed analysis of capitalist practices and the other is a personal memoir, both depend on the ideology that pits sales against art.

Berman's critique contrasts commercial publishing with an

idealized vision of what might have occurred in a precapitalist economy of patronage. He argues that since commercial publishers treat writers as employees rather than colleagues (62), the loss of a personal connection between author and publisher causes language to appear "decoupled from both expression and discourse" (64). While I agree that publishing institutions have a significant effect on literature, Berman's claim that friendship between author and patron once produced more authentic expression and discourse ignores the disadvantages of patronage. The need to please a particular patron can be more restricting than the market, and the absence of a need to please anyone else can limit the writer's audience.

Berman himself provides evidence that authors rather than publishers wanted to break the personal connection: he points out that a German writers' union established in 1879 "rejected the traditional assumption that authors betrayed their authentic calling if they began to worry about their financial status" (67). The dichotomy of art and money was so invidious that authors themselves challenged it. Similarly, British writers hired literary agents and willingly paid the agent's usual fee of 10 percent. Publishers vehemently objected to the loss of the personal bond because it operated in their favor. Some publishers simply refused to deal with agents, accusing authors of betraying old friendships by seeking the highest price for their manuscripts.[4]

Berman conceives of the writer as a proletarian whose labor is appropriated by the publisher: the author "experiences the social distribution of his work as expropriation" (66). Although popularity reduced critical esteem, there is no sign that writers objected to sales as expropriation. Berman protests publishers' profits, yet he believes that authors should be paid: "Certainly authors, like everyone else, have always had to find a way to survive" (55). He implies that a person develops the aspiration to become something called an "author" before there is a system that pays for manuscripts. But the possibility of "surviving" by one's writing improved with the growth of commercial publishing. A literary market had to exist before one could be a professional author, that is, before one could earn a living by selling one's writing. When Berman contrasts "precapitalist forms of remuneration (patronage) and the characteristically capitalist dependence on the market and the publisher (especially in the form of royalties)" (55), he does not consider the extent to which the market gives the writer a measure of professional independence.

The development of literary agencies, however, suggests that authors realized they had strong financial interests and assets. If authors are considered fungible workers, the average price becomes an index of value, but writers recognized the value of individual reputation in developing what might be called brand-name recognition. In this sense, the self-promotion of authors and the parallels between their lives and their fiction contributed to the market value of their signatures. Seeing that authorship was profitable, required little capital, and offered more independence than most jobs, many people tried to write novels. As the market grew, more writers competed for publication, and more books competed for buyers. Publishers made money, but so did authors.

Berman argues that the relationship between the publisher and the author, not readers' preferences, determines the kind of fiction that enters the market: "authors who understand themselves as employees dependent on publishing houses with precise marketing strategies will choose to write in certain ways. In other words, it is not the growth of the readership but the constraints on the writers, not democracy but capitalism which leads to Ganghofer and other proponents of pulp fiction" (56). Adopting Theodor Adorno's distinction between the interests of the "culture industry" and those of the popular audience, Berman absolves readers of bad taste. If people buy pulp fiction, the culture industry is responsible. Berman contends that when publishers forced authors to write for a large audience, literature became a commodity and readers became mass market consumers. Thus, bestsellers lacked any aesthetic value and assumed a reactionary purpose (66).

Seeing the popular book as a commodity, Berman questions the author's sincerity; if it sells, it is not art. Again, his assumption that the qualities that make a book popular cannot be aesthetic illustrates the ideological dichotomy between art and money. He lacks Henry James's appreciation of a range of aesthetic responses. In my view, the inability of the elite author to imagine a wide audience, like the failure of the popular author to appeal to an elite audience, was a result of the diversification of the audience. Berman is as elitist as Q. D. Leavis in seeing this expansion as degradation rather than democratization. Unwilling to posit differences in aesthetic taste and response, Berman asserts that the mass market has no aesthetic reaction and, like Adorno, blames the culture industry for destroying the chimera called authentic popular taste.

Although Berman's ideal publisher emerges from a Marxist perspective, Siegfried Unseld resembles this ideal. Unseld aligns himself with patrons and apologizes for his business interests. He advocates a personal relationship between publisher and author and urges other publishers to build their reputations by developing lists of esteemed authors. Parading his contempt for money, Unseld tries to excuse his concern with profit: "We need a strong financial basis primarily in order to be able to remain independent and to assure our authors as much independence as possible" (36). Like Benjamin and Adorno, whom he cites approvingly, Unseld believes that seeking profit is inimical to art. He justifies his profits by promising to use them to assist artists.

For Unseld, the writer who is a true artist follows an inner program, and the publisher dutifully promotes it. Unseld explains that he learned his proper role from James Joyce's credo of self-sacrifice. Quoting Joyce's allusion to *Faust,* "Ich bin der [*sic*] Fleisch der stets bejaht,"[5] Unseld pays tribute to this stance: "I have never read a more extreme formulation of a writer's longing" (23). Yet Unseld's faith falters when he defines this aesthetic commitment. First, he attributes it to the author's search for *"his own truth"* (20), but then he suggests that perhaps mental illness is at work: "The author centers his confidence in the person who respects creativity but who also knows that a source of that creativity often lies in illness, in neurosis" (34). His awe of the artist barely conceals the condescension evident in his description of the publisher's role: "he has to be something of a literary midwife, a psychoanalyst, a businessman, and a patron of the arts" (37). Minimizing the importance of financial interests, Unseld's professional credo also depends on the ideology of art and money that ruled modernists.

Although authors could not know who their readers were, thanks to the popular press, readers knew more and more about authors.

Publicity reduced the distance between author and reader and miti-gated the inaccessibility of modernist fiction. As my epigraph from *Immortality* illustrates, even a postmodernist like Milan Kundera real-izes that readers want to know as much as possible about authors' lives. We want to believe that fiction reveals lived experience, and Kundera dramatizes the persistence of our search for the life behind the text.

The public was acquainted with the personae of many modernist authors before reading their books. Each of the authors I consider benefited from publicity about his life, despite his intention to make his fiction impersonal. Conrad was the trilingual expatriate seaman who had adventured into the Congo and the South Seas. Joyce was the bohemian artist who had defied social, political, and literary con-ventions to create. Lawrence was the prophet of eroticism who had foreseen the ravages of industrialization. These personae fascinated the public and generated interest in novels that could be read as auto-biographical accounts of the writers' lives. Yet even the most per-sonal text is the product of cultural forces operating on the author, the audience, and the circumstances of publication; thus, the authors' personae were themselves products of literary institutions.

A major source of publicity for modernism was prosecution for obscenity. The trials of *Ulysses* and *The Rainbow* are often portrayed as battles between creative genius and repressive conventions, a con-flict consistent with the governing ideology of the artist. But con-trary to magistrates' motives, these prosecutions had the effect of advertising banned books beyond the public that might otherwise have been expected to buy or read them. Formal complexity allowed modernist authors to defend the erotic aspects of their work as art rather than pornography, while the erotic content attracted readers. Joyce and Lawrence demonstrated that sexually explicit fiction could attack bourgeois values yet attract bourgeois readers. After these pros-ecutions, to be considered modern, a writer had to address sexual issues as well as formal questions. To varying degrees, other mod-ernists, including Ford Madox Ford, Wyndham Lewis, Jean Rhys, Virginia Woolf, and Djuna Barnes, adopted the same solution to the dilemma of authorship they inherited.

Joyce portrays the impact of the press in *Ulysses*. Set in a newspaper office, the "Aeolus" chapter parodies the format and style of a daily paper. Stephen agrees to use his influence with an editor to help Mr. Deasy get publicity by publishing a letter (27). The editor is indignant at the request, but the letter appears. Similarly, Bloom wants the paper to "puff" one of his advertisers in its news columns. The editor's response is righteous indignation: "—Will you tell him he can kiss my arse?" (120). Bloom repeats his request, gets the same answer, and disregards it: "While Mr Bloom stood weighing the point and about to smile he strode on jerkily" (121). Apparently Bloom has heard this bluster before.

Although the editor compromises his principles, he and Stephen both believe that writing should be disinterested. Asking Stephen to write for the paper, the editor echoes Joyce's account of his commission to write the first stories of *Dubliners*. The headline of this section is "YOU CAN DO IT":

> —I want you to write something for me, he said. Something with a bite in it. You can do it. I see it in your face. (111)

Despite the mockery the headline conveys, the editor's confidence in Stephen's talent and his own ability to detect it characterizes the ideology of authorship they hold in common. The hack may need to show his wares to sell them, but the artist does not deign to provide evidence of genius.

This ideology demands contempt for money. Stephen finds the need for money so degrading that as he pockets his pay, he reflects: "Symbols too of beauty and of power. A lump in my pocket: symbols soiled by greed and misery" (25). His attitude contrasts with Bloom's attempt to find a reasonable solution to Stephen's dilemma. Knowing that Stephen needs time to write and a way to support himself, Bloom provides the kind of practical advice neither Stephen nor Joyce could accept:

> Added to which of course would be the pecuniary emolument by no means to be sneezed at, going hand in hand with his tuition fees. Not, he parenthesised, that for the sake of filthy lucre he need necessarily embrace the lyric platform as a walk in life for any lengthy space of time. But a step in the required direction it was beyond yea or nay and both monetarily and mentally it contained no reflection on his

dignity in the smallest and it often turned in uncommonly handy to be handed a cheque at a muchneeded moment when every little helped. . . . And it need not detract from the other by one iota as, being his own master, he would have heaps of time to practise liter-ature in his spare moments when desirous of so doing without its clashing with his vocal career or containing anything derogatory whatsoever as it was a matter for himself alone. (542)

Bloom anticipates Stephen's objections to "filthy lucre" as well as his desire to maintain his "dignity" and to remain "his own master," but he reasonably argues that a check will give Stephen "heaps of time to practise literature in his spare moments when desirous of doing so." Patronage saved Joyce from making such an accommodation, and it allowed him to satirize Bloom's practicality.

   Lawrence also recognized the importance of publicity in the lit-erary market. In *Lady Chatterley's Lover,* for example, Lawrence makes Michaelis, the Irish playwright who becomes Lady Chatterley's lover early in the novel, a master of public relations. Clifford Chatterley's eagerness to learn how to promote his own literary for-tunes brings Connie Chatterley and Michaelis together. Connie's judgment of Clifford indicates that Lawrence understood the con-nections between critical acclaim, personal publicity, and sales. Connie scathingly analyzes Clifford's combination of clever writing and self-promotion:

His seemed the most modern of modern voices, with his uncanny, lame instinct for publicity he had become, in four or five years, one of the best-known of the young "intellectuals." Where the intellect came in, Connie did not quite see. Clifford was really clever at that slightly humorous analysis of people and motives which leaves every-thing in bits at the end. (50)

Connie is even more contemptuous of Clifford's desire for acclaim than his desire to make money:

Clifford, of course, had still many childish taboos and fetishes. He wanted to be thought "really good." Which was all cock-a-whoopy nonsense. What was really good was what actually caught on. It was no good being really good, and getting left with it. It seemed as if most of the "really good" men just missed the bus. After all, you only lived one life: and if you missed the bus, you just were left on the pavement, along with the rest of the failures. (63)

Connie's scorn for the alliance between critical acclaim and its pay-off is part of her revulsion at Clifford's lack of vitality. Although her tone is cynical, her claim that what is really good is what is popular expresses a truth about canon formation: neither acclaim without sales nor sales without acclaim can establish a book's literary value. Her pragmatism violates the ideology that separates money and art, but it addresses the quandary of the unsuccessful novelist who cannot know if he is an unacknowledged genius or one more aspiring amateur "left on the pavement."

"Who Paid for Modernism?" is a crass question because it also violates the ideology that polarizes money and art. I have posed it, however, because money haunted modernist novelists as a stigma and as a reward. While the literal answer to the question is that patrons, agents, and publishers paid authors, there is also a figurative answer. Authors paid for modernism by giving up the wide audience their ambition desired and their talent deserved.

Notes

Introduction

1. The relationship between writers' lives and their work is ordinarily the province of biography, but most biographies emphasize what is unique rather than what is common in a writer's experience. In contrast to biographers, Lucien Goldmann distinguishes the "individual significant function" a work has for its author from the cultural forces that govern "the truly literary character of the work." He proposes that "the sociologist of literature—and, in general, the critic—must treat the conscious intentions of the author as one indication among many others, as a sort of reflection on the work, from which he gathers suggestions, in the same way as any other critical work, but on which he must form his judgment in the light of the text, without according it any favor" (586–87). He regards the author not as a unique individual but as one whose behavior has a "historical character (of which all cultural creation forms part) which has a transindividual subject" (588). Goldmann opposes psychological explanations of literature not only because the author's private self is unknowable, but also because they fail to account for the text as a whole or for the specifically literary aspects of the text (596–97). In contrast to poststructuralists, Goldmann treats the author as a factor worth interpreting as a representative of his or her culture. For cultural critics like Pierre Bourdieu and Alain Viala, literature is a product of cultural forces operating in a field that obviously includes authors and readers, but also depends on agents, publishers, critics, and reviewers.

2. While Joyce and Lawrence present the most extreme and influential claims of martyrdom to illustrate Poggioli's point, other modernist writers faced similar publishing obstacles, though specifics naturally differ.

3. Following Bourdieu, Alain Viala empirically relates the reception of a text to the position of its author, and he analyzes this interaction in an inventory of the mediations or "prismatic effects" that operate in the literary field. These mediations are interposed between the "social referent

and the text as well as between the work and its readers" (Viala 563). The author's relation to the work is another part: Viala argues that although the writer's personal life is insignificant, an author's career enters the literary field as a major force through a "trajectory" of positions. Viala accepts the importance of the author's reputation:

> The moment a writer is recognized as such in society by publications, the capital so constituted weighs on each subsequent creation; to redo or continue what has already been done or else to break this trend amounts to being judged on the basis of and through the image of the writer and other preexisting images. Thus, even when unconscious, the choices of forms, referents, manners, and possible explicit statements acquire meaning only in relationship to the range of images that can be examined, just as each text can be understood in relation to this series of representations. (Viala 571)

4. Accepted as standard works, the biographies by Frederic Karl, Richard Ellmann, and Harry T. Moore continue to influence criticism. Karl's biography of Conrad was published in 1979; the first volume of Conrad's *Collected Letters*, which Karl edited, did not begin to appear until 1983. Ellmann's biography of Joyce was published in 1959; the three-volume set of Joyce's letters, the last two volumes edited by Ellmann, did not appear until 1966. Ellmann's 1982 *New and Revised Edition* of his biography incorporated much of this material. Moore's *The Intelligent Heart* was published in 1954; his edition of Lawrence's letters appeared in 1962. Moore's revised biography, *The Priest of Love,* appeared in 1974. The Cambridge edition of Lawrence's letters, edited by James T. Boulton, began to appear in 1979. John Worthen's multivolume biography benefits from the Cambridge edition and gives more attention to Lawrence's commercial interests than Moore does.

5. The prominence of publishing business in the correspondence of Joyce has been noticed. See Richard F. Peterson and Alan M. Cohn, "James Job: The Critical Reception of Joyce's Letters" in *James Joyce Quarterly* 19 (1982), 429–40.

Chapter One

1. See Chapters 3 and 4. Discussing Gothic fiction written a century earlier, Bradford K. Mudge argues that the metaphor of prostitution for popular literature was rooted in gender stereotypes about its writers and readers and that critical opposition to Gothic fiction was an attempt to "normalize female sexuality along middle-class lines" (94).

2. E.L.A., in "James Joyce to his Literary Agents," dissents from Sylvia Beach's report that Joyce thought *Ulysses* "would interest very few readers and he never counted on any financial return from it" (Ford 32).

3. Bourdieu notes that Flaubert and his contemporaries in the art for art's sake movement came from financially secure families: "In brief, it was still (inherited) money that assured freedom from money" (553). In contrast, both Joyce and Lawrence rose in social status via the avant-garde link between the wealthy and the talented.

4. The range of the audience also made it difficult for modernists to alter their work to suit readers. Analyzing the development of literary professionalism in this period, Louis Menand locates the source of the serious artist's rhetorical position in the author's inability to conceive of the reader. He recounts a vignette from Oscar Wilde's trial to demonstrate the result of this failure:

> "I have no knowledge of the views of ordinary individuals," he replied during one of his trials to a question about the effect *Dorian Gray* might be expected to have on the views of the ordinary reader. "You did not prevent the ordinary individual from buying your book?" returned his cross-examiner. "I have never discouraged him" was Wilde's response. Wilde's replies cover both ends of the professionalist contradiction: as a practitioner, Wilde was naturally indifferent to the interests of his readers, but as a businessman, so to speak, he saw that indifference was a pose that would sell books. The exchange shows the aestheticist attitude at its most clairvoyant. It seems to see right through to the time when an apparent contempt for the views of the audience would be a chief ingredient of artistic success, the sign that the artist really cares. (Menand 116–17)

Unable to identify his readers, Wilde made indifference to readers his overt rhetorical stance. Menand argues that refusing to consider the reader's response became a mark of respect for the reader.

5. Plentiful evidence appears in the published letters of Conrad and Lewis and the unpublished letters of Pain, Williamson, and many others in the Pinker Archive. See, for example, Conrad quoted by Garnett (9); letter from Lewis to Pinker (Rose 43–44); letter from Pain to Pinker, 16 July 1909, Pinker Collection; and letter from Amalgamated Press to Eric Pinker, 4 May 1928.

6. This was written before tax laws penalized backlists, but more recent confirmation comes from Ray Walters: "Much of the spirit and some of the procedures of the cottage industry that characterized publishing early in this century will return. The number of publishing houses will multiply" (12).

7. Lawrence S. Rainey makes a similar point in his analysis of the publication of *The Waste Land:* "Patronage could nurture literary modernism only to the threshold of its confrontation with a wider public; beyond that point, it would require commercial success to ratify its viability as a significant idiom" (286).

8. Michael Lane graphs "Typical Sales Patterns of Books" (35).

9. Leslie Fiedler explicates this process in an idiosyncratic combination of introspection and literary history in *What Was Literature?* He speculates that every writer needs publication, and money is the most reliable "token that one has in fact touched, moved, shared one's most private fantasies with the faceless, nameless 'you' to whom the writer's all-too-familiar 'I' longs to be joined in mutual pleasure." Although his work "remains incomplete until it has passed from the desk to the marketplace," the writer feels guilty for selling a product of his soul. His guilt "breeds resentment against the intermediaries and accomplices who have made possible what he himself has desired" (24). Therefore, he projects his anger at himself onto publishers. Fiedler's attempt at depth psychology of authors may lack a clinical foundation, but it explains the almost ubiquitous tendency of writers to complain about publishers.

10. Peter Rabinowitz notes the importance of publishing practices to readers: "One of the reasons that it is easier to read texts that have been published than those which have not is that the knowledge that the text has passed through editors helps assure us that this rule [that it can be seen as an example of or a variation of *some* preexisting genre category or plot type] has been adhered to" (118n).

11. In "Fiction and the Erotic Cover," John Sutherland shows that when these works were issued in paperback format, publishers deliberately tried to sell serious literature through sexy cover art: "Predictably, the back cover stresses the obscenity and persecution of the 'Author of *Ulysses*'" (14), and "The back cover of *Women in Love* harps predictably on the banned-book aspect of the novel" (16).

Chapter Two

1. I have used the Cambridge University Press edition of *The Collected Letters of Joseph Conrad*, hereafter indicated by *Letters* and the volume and page number. References to Frederic Karl's biography of Conrad will be indicated by Karl's name and the page number.

2. "When Conrad was particularly pleased with his work he pooh-poohed it in his letters—'This is the sort of rot I am writing now,' he says for example about *Heart of Darkness* " (Garnett 27). Garnett warns that Conrad's letters cannot always be read literally: "I must add a word here

about Conrad's play of irony. He was so perfect an artist in the expression of his moods and feelings that it needed a fine ear to seize the blended shades of friendly derision, flattery, self-depreciation, sardonic criticism and affection in his tone" (20).

3. See Michael Levenson (31–36) on Conrad's subjectivist epistemology.

4. For this support, Karl reports, Conrad returned slurs, "portraying him as the stereotypical Hebrew tight with money and deceptive in business affairs" (379). Conrad regarded Unwin as a "dominating, possessive type of person" and mocked him by "drawing attention to his Jewishness" (337). A few years later in *The Inheritors,* Conrad and Ford Madox Ford (who changed his name from Hueffer during World War I) portrayed Unwin as Polehampton, "a cultural ignoramus for whom books were simply marketable commodities" (Karl 379). While dissatisfied authors often portrayed publishers as philistines, this stereotype adds prejudice to the dichotomy between art and money.

5. Fredric Jameson also sees Marlow performing this function but considers it reactionary: "The representational fiction of a storytelling situation organized around Marlow marks the vain attempt to conjure back the older unity of the literary institution" before it was disrupted by "market relations" (219–20).

6. Karl comments, "This situation was bound to blow up in his dealings with Pinker, for underlying Conrad's hatred of the common marketplace was the fact that it was, at least partially, run by Jews to make money for Jews—what he had characterized to Graham as the 'shent-per-shent business'—and Pinker was a feed-in of material to that very market" (524). Feeling trapped, he lashed out in anti-Semitic stereotypes, an ugly variation on the tendency of many writers to insult publishers as philistines. Nevertheless, when a review of *Under Western Eyes* compared the narrator to a Jew, Conrad misread this point as a hint that he was a Jew. He associated himself with the narrator and expressed his outrage: "I believe that some time ago that preposterous Papist Belloc has been connecting me with Father Abraham, whether to hurt me or to serve me, or simply because he's an idiot—I don't know." Although irritated at the inaccuracy, he protested: "I trust I have no contemptible prejudices against any kind of human beings . . ." (*Letters* 4:486).

Chapter Three

1. Quoted in Ellmann (559). The object of scorn in this ditty was A. S. W. Rosenbach, a collector who purchased the manuscript of *Ulysses,* sold at auction by John Quinn, for $1,975 in 1924. Joyce tried to buy the

manuscript back from Rosenbach, who countered with an offer to buy the corrected page proofs as well. Joyce wrote these lines to Harriet Weaver to express his contempt for the business.

2. In contrast to my interpretation of Russell's letter, Magalaner and Kain describe it as "an almost rude letter" (54). Their reaction indicates their contempt for rhetorical concerns, as their next comment indicates: "Yet this was just what Joyce could not do, then or later" (54).

3. Tracing the stages of modernism, Michael Levenson notes that it valued clarity before obscurity: "Though subjective, then, the serious artist is scientific in his subjectivity and the 'more precise his record the more lasting and unassailable his work of art.' Thus to symbolist 'evocation,' Imagism opposed precision, hardness, clarity of outline" (120). By the end of World War I, however, the modernist aesthetic shifted to "a consciousness of fragmentation" (192). The artist's duty to select became a compulsion to multiply, as meaning became "the product of multiple perspectives" (184), and the work of art developed "not by resolving conflicts but by enlarging contexts" (201).

4. See Chester G. Anderson. Riquelme also addresses the difficulty of knowing if Stephen is the narrator (51–52) and lists contributions to the debate on aesthetic distance through the late seventies (250, n. 7).

5. Rabinowitz warns, "If one assumes that all features of a text are to receive close attention from an interpreter, then a text . . . becomes an infinite and impenetrable web of relationships. In the end, such a view not only makes everything equally important, but also makes everything equally unimportant: only boredom can result" (51).

6. In contrast, Bernard Benstock argues that Joyce's troubles with *Dubliners* drove Joyce from an Irish readership to a "truly international audience" drawn from "the mainstream of European thought" (223–24).

7. These terms are given in the 1959 edition of Ellmann's biography (615), but the second edition merely states: "During the last several months he had been receiving offers steadily for both *Finnegans Wake* and *Ulysses*" (641).

8. "He appears to have succeeded very well."

Chapter Four

1. Citations from the Cambridge edition of *The Collected Letters of D. H. Lawrence* are indicated by Boulton, the volume number, and the page number.

2. More than most of Lawrence's critics, John Worthen respects Lawrence's explicit statements of rhetorical intention. Linking Lawrence's theory of fiction to specific rhetorical objectives in *D. H. Lawrence and the*

Idea of the Novel, Worthen argues that from the beginning of his career, Lawrence was writing for the reader, not for himself. Although Worthen attributes the quality of Lawrence's best work to the depth of his "engagement," he allows rhetorical intention and formal control, rather than deep feeling alone, to count as evidence of engagement. Worthen's more recent *D. H. Lawrence: The Early Years* pays attention to the cultural models of authorship that influenced Lawrence (131).

3. See Draper, *D. H. Lawrence: The Critical Heritage,* 33–35.

4. Worthen attributes these weaknesses to "Lawrence's problem with finding a public voice as a novelist. . . . I suggest that the same failure to be confident of a public voice lies behind the cloying metaphorical habit, too. . . . His use of the first person in his fiction was nearly always a failure, and none of his other novels employ it" (*Idea* 13). Worthen is excluding Lawrence's use of the intrusive narrator in *Mr Noon* and its intermittent use in *Aaron's Rod* and *Kangaroo.* Worthen blames these problems on Lawrence's effort to be "literary": "He had to learn a way of making a novel that, without being a copy of other novels, could actually address itself to an audience. He also had to learn, by trying, whether the audience whose appreciation he aimed for in *The White Peacock* was really the audience he wanted. But it is, too, important to register that he had the ambition of writing for an audience from the start" (*Idea* 14).

5. Born Frieda von Richthofen, she also was connected to Max Weber and Alfred Weber through her sister. Martin Green describes the women's own intellectual achievements and independent lives in *The von Richthofen Sisters.*

6. Robyn Warhol distinguishes engaging from distancing narrators in nineteenth-century fiction, emphasizing the relationship between the implied reader stipulated in the text and the actual reader to gauge distance. In either case, the presence of direct address functions as apostrophe.

7. Shari Benstock offers a postmodernist reading of apostrophe in *Finnegans Wake:* "Apostrophe signals at once a radical interiority (the address is inward, not outward) and fragmentation. As represented subjectivity, the voice is disembodied, divided, echoing on the wind" (65).

8. Carol Siegel notes that the "oppositional female voices" are "unanswerable" and that Lawrence affirms the point of view of his female characters when it contradicts that of the "Lawrence" character (8–10).

9. Philip Sicker argues that in contrast to the formal control of Henry James, James Joyce, and Thomas Mann, Lawrence's interpretation of the "artist's need to separate his personality from his work" focused on the effort to "let real objects live in their own 'objective substance.'" Instead of the invisible author, in the novels of the 1920s Lawrence prefers the "straightforward manipulation and unabashed sermonizing of a fully dramatized narrator" (203).

10. *Mr Noon* was recognized as a forerunner of postmodernist fiction in a special issue of *The D. H. Lawrence Review* (Summer 1988) and in Earl G. Ingersoll's "D. H. Lawrence's *Mr Noon* as a Postmodern Text."

11. Philip Sicker makes a similar point: "Fielding's narrator encourages us to be collaborators in their good deeds and to laugh at pride and pomposity by appealing to our sagacity, memory, and sense of decency. Lawrence's moral aims, though different, are no less tendentious: but instead of being cast as enlightened supporters, we are charged with smugness and stupidity. *Mr Noon* seems, at first, not a dialogue but a harangue aimed at the reader, who is himself the object of satire" (205).

12. Baker notes that the narrator also penetrates the subjectivity of Aaron's wife: "We may perhaps object quite rightly that the point of view at times shifts erratically and awkwardly from Aaron to Lottie to the narrator, but this complexity is clearly a part of Lawrence's intentions, his refusal to explain in simplified terms what is after all a very subtle and intricate matter" (155).

13. Paul Baker responds to critics' objections to this kind of intrusion:

> What many critics fail to observe is that Lawrence is perfectly *aware* of the awkwardness of the device and cannot resist poking fun at those very novels which he is imitating, particularly in the early chapters of the novel. The use of the fussy and sententious narrator . . . is thus simply a humorous parody of other similar yet delightful intrusions of early "narrators" in English fiction— most noticeably in the novels of Fielding, Dickens or Thackeray. The use of the archaic device is also part of Lawrence's satiric attacks upon English notions of what is proper in art as well as life. (163)

Baker rightly points out the inadequacy of approaches that focus on the novel's autobiographical episodes or social criticism. He argues that as fiction, the novel has a thematic unity that justifies the variety of formal techniques Lawrence uses: "This unity may be perceived if we are able to step back momentarily, as it were, setting aside our notions of what a novel should or should not be, to consider in isolation the scheme of debates which occur throughout the novel" (Baker 167). While it is impossible to set aside all notions of what a novel should be, in the context of postmodernism, this novel does not need to be evaluated according to norms of unity.

14. Rick Rylance emphasizes the ways the ironic mode undercuts all political convictions: "The book is an ideological hall-of-mirrors typical of Lawrence's fictional procedures. . . . What this difficult dialectical method does to the politics of a novel like *Kangaroo* is to scupper any

sense of a firm solution. The form of the book reflects this. It is tellingly non-linear in narrative, and moves disconcertingly in time, tone and perspective. . . . Yet the tone is not merely dismayed, for the book is written in a mode of Romantic irony usually associated with Byron or Keats; that is, *Kangaroo* subverts, yet understands, its ironically conceived central character's predicament and unsteady venturing" (171).

15. Marianna Torgovnick notes that Lawrence regenders the primitive from women in *Women in Love* to men in *The Plumed Serpent:* "The association now of 'the primitive' with masculinity is crucial, I believe, in the turn Lawrence's version of the primitive takes from the degenerative to the regenerative" (163).

16. Pinkney also notes the echoes of *Heart of Darkness* in *The Plumed Serpent,* though he emphasizes the contrasting formal expression of similar themes in the two works (159–62).

17. Joan D. Peters disputes the claim that the novel is merely a return to conventional realism and a nineteenth century narrator (19). Although the narrative is "scrupulously limited to the point of view of individual characters," she points out, the narrator intrudes once in the center of the book to provide a "structural blueprint" (5): "Therefore the novel, properly handled, can reveal the most secret places of life: for it is in the *passional* secret places of life, above all, that the tide of sensitive awareness needs to ebb and flow, cleansing and freshening" (*Lady Chatterley* 101). Peters distinguishes this authorial voice from the voices of all the other characters.

Chapter Five

1. Benjamin writes: "Es ist also eine Lebensbedingung des Epischen im neuen Sinne, dies Private, aus welchem der Roman sein Recht nimmt, zu liquidieren [It is thus a necessity of the new epic that this privateness from which the novel takes its justification be eliminated]" (310). Russell A. Berman cites this passage (77).

2. Patrick Brantlinger notes the convergence of left and right in their opposition to mass culture.

3. As Thomas Strychacz explains, "A mass audience of readers, James perceives, exists more as theory than as fact, and the exigencies of twentieth-century publishing have indeed shown that financial success depends on reaching a specific, well-defined group of readers—one of many mass audiences—rather than aiming at some amorphous mass readership. . . . Writing specifically for one subdivision of the chessboard mass audience, the literary writer may restrict but simultaneously guarantee the salability

of any piece of writing" (21). Strychacz expands this point in his discussion of the American literary market:

> Models of literary production that describe the hegemony of the mass market thus seem inadequate on at least four counts. First, they oversimplify writers' attitudes toward mass culture, the mass market, and the desirability of reaching a huge audience. Second, as a corollary, they fail to account for the impulse toward esoteric writing strategies in many writers (including those commonly labeled naturalist) who underwent an "apprenticeship" to journalism. Third, they ignore the particular way these strategies incorporate and subvert the languages, forms, and ideologies specific to mass culture. Fourth, and perhaps most important, they fail to recognize ways in which writers might maintain cultural hegemony in spite of widespread perceptions about the dominance of mass culture. By focusing on the mass market, in other words, these studies ignore the fact that the newly forming structures of the marketplace allowed for a special kind of esoteric writing and, what is more important, made it possible for this kind of writing to assume cultural authority. (20)

4. For example, in 1906 the editor of the *Saturday Review* was still refusing to deal with literary agents, and clients told Pinker that publishers offered them better terms if they would cancel their contract with the agency.

5. "I am the flesh that always affirms," whereas Mephistopheles says, "I am the spirit that always negates."

Works Cited

Anderson, Chester G. "Controversy: The Question of Esthetic Distance."
In *A Portrait of the Artist as a Young Man: Text, Criticism, and Notes,*
edited by Chester G. Anderson, 446–54. Viking Critical Library
Edition. New York: Penguin, 1985.

Arcana, Judith. "I Remember Mama: Mother Blaming in *Sons and
Lovers.*" *The D. H. Lawrence Review* 21 (1990): 137–51.

Baker, Paul G. *A Reassessment of D. H. Lawrence's "Aaron's Rod."* Ann
Arbor, Mich.: UMI Research Press, 1983.

Barthes, Roland. "From Work to Text." In *Textual Strategies,* edited by
Josue V. Harari, 73–81. Ithaca, N.Y.: Cornell University Press,
1979.

————. *Writing Degree Zero.* Translated by Annette Lavers and Colin
Smith. New York: Hill and Wang, 1968.

Benjamin, Walter. "Oskar Maria Graf als Erzähler." In *Gesammelte
Schriften.* Vol. 3, 309–11. Frankfurt am Main: Suhrkamp, 1972.

Benstock, Bernard. "The Assassin and the Censor: Political and Literary
Tensions." *Clio* 11 (1982): 219–38.

Benstock, Shari. *Textualizing the Feminine: On the Limits of Genre.* Norman
and London: University of Oklahoma Press, 1991.

Berman, Russell A. *Modern Culture and Critical Theory: Art, Politics, and the
Legacy of the Frankfurt School.* Madison: University of Wisconsin
Press, 1989.

Blackburn, William, ed. *Joseph Conrad: Letters to William Blackwood and
David S. Meldrum.* Durham, N.C.: Duke University Press, 1958.

Boulton, James T. et al, eds. *The Letters of D. H. Lawrence.* 7 vols.
Cambridge: Cambridge University Press, 1979–93.

Bourdieu, Pierre. "Flaubert's Point of View." Translated by Priscilla
Parkhurst Ferguson. *Critical Inquiry* 14 (1988): 539–62.

Bradbury, Malcolm. *The Social Context of Modern English Literature.* New
York: Schocken, 1971.

Brantlinger, Patrick. *Bread and Circuses: Theories of Mass Culture as Social Decay.* Ithaca, N.Y.: Cornell University Press, 1983.

Britton, Derek. *Lady Chatterley: The Making of the Novel.* London: Unwin Hyman, 1988.

Clark, L. D. *Dark Night of the Body: D. H. Lawrence's "The Plumed Serpent."* Austin: University of Texas Press, 1964.

Conrad, Joseph. *Almayer's Folly and Tales of Unrest.* London: John Grant, 1925.

————. *Chance.* Garden City, New York: Doubleday, 1924.

————. *The Collected Letters of Joseph Conrad.* 5 vols. Edited by Frederick R. Karl and Laurence Davies. Cambridge: Cambridge University Press, 1983–96.

————. *The Nigger of the "Narcissus."* Garden City, N.Y.: Doubleday, 1914.

————. "An Outpost of Progress." In *Tales of the East and West,* edited by Morton Dauwen Zabel, 214–33. Garden City, N.Y.: Hanover House, 1958.

Daleski, H. M. "The Son and the Artist." In *D. H. Lawrence's "Sons and Lovers,"* edited by Harold Bloom, 23–46. New York: Chelsea House, 1988.

Draper, R. P., ed. *D. H. Lawrence: The Critical Heritage.* London and Boston: Routledge and Kegan Paul, 1970.

"Dubliners." Unpublished reader's report for Grant Richards, Houghton Library, Harvard University.

E.L.A. "James Joyce to His Literary Agents." *More Books* (Bulletin of the Boston Public Library) 18 (1943): 22.

Eliot, T. S. "The Metaphysical Poets." In *Selected Prose of T. S. Eliot,* edited by Frank Kermode, 59–67. New York: Harcourt Brace Jovanovich, 1975.

————. "Reflections on Contemporary Poetry I." *The Egoist* 4 (1917): 118–19.

————. "*Ulysses,* Order, and Myth." In *Selected Prose of T. S. Eliot,* edited by Frank Kermode, 175–78. New York: Harcourt Brace Jovanovich, 1975.

Ellmann, Richard. *James Joyce: New and Revised Edition.* New York: Oxford University Press, 1982.

Escarpit, Robert. *The Book Revolution.* London: George G. Harrap, 1966.

————. "The Act of Publication: Publication and Creation." In *The Sociology of Art and Literature,* edited by Milton C. Albrecht, James H. Barnett, and Mason Griff, 396–406. New York: Praeger, 1970.

Feather, John. *A History of British Publishing.* London: Croom Helm, 1988.

Fiedler, Leslie. *What Was Literature?* New York: Simon and Schuster, 1982.

Flaubert, Gustave. *Selected Letters of Gustave Flaubert.* Translated and edited by Francis Steegmuller. New York: Farrar, Straus and Young, 1953.

Ford, Hugh. *Published in Paris.* New York: Macmillan, 1975.

Foucault, Michel. "What Is an Author?" In *Textual Strategies,* edited by Josue V. Harari, 141–60. Ithaca, N.Y.: Cornell University Press, 1979.

Freud, Sigmund. "Creative Writers and Day-Dreaming." In *Standard Edition,* translated and edited by James Strachey, vol. 9, 143–53. London: Hogarth, 1959.

Garnett, Edward, ed. *Letters from Joseph Conrad, 1895 to 1924.* New York: Bobbs-Merrill, 1928.

Goldmann, Lucien. "The Sociology of Literature: Status and Problems of Method." In *The Sociology of Art and Literature,* edited by Milton C. Albrecht, James H. Barnett, and Mason Griff, 582–609. New York: Praeger, 1970.

Green, Martin. *The von Richthofen Sisters.* New York: Basic Books, 1974.

Hepburn, James, ed. *Letters of Arnold Bennett.* Vol. 1. London: Oxford University Press, 1966.

Hoffman, Frederick J. "Lawrence's Quarrel with Freud." In *D. H. Lawrence and "Sons and Lovers": Sources and Criticism,* edited by E. W. Tedlock, Jr., 101–11. New York: New York University Press, 1965.

Hough, Graham. *The Dark Sun.* New York: Macmillan, 1957.

Howe, Irving. "The Culture of Modernism." In *Decline of the New,* 3–33. New York: Harcourt, Brace and World, 1963.

Hyde, H. Montgomery. *The Lady Chatterley's Lover Trial.* London: The Bodley Head, 1990.

Ingersoll, Earl G. "D. H. Lawrence's *Mr. Noon* as a Postmodern Text." *Modern Language Review* 85 (1990): 304–9.

Iser, Wolfgang. *The Implied Reader.* Baltimore and London: Johns Hopkins University Press, 1974.

James, Henry. "The Question of the Opportunities." In *Literary Criticism,* 651–57. New York: Library of America, 1984.

Jameson, Fredric. *The Political Unconscious.* Ithaca, N.Y.: Cornell University Press, 1981.

Johnson, Barbara. *A World of Difference.* Baltimore and London: Johns Hopkins University Press, 1987.

Joyce, James. *Letters of James Joyce.* Vol. 1. Edited by Stuart Gilbert. Vols. 2 and 3. Edited by Richard Ellmann. New York: Viking, 1966.

———. *A Portrait of the Artist as a Young Man.* New York: Viking, 1964.

———. *Selected Letters of James Joyce.* Edited by Richard Ellmann. New York: Viking, 1975.

————. *Ulysses*. Edited by Hans Walter Gabler. New York: Vintage, 1986.

Karl, Frederick R. *Joseph Conrad: The Three Lives*. New York: Farrar, Straus and Giroux, 1979.

Kenner, Hugh. *Joyce's Voices*. Berkeley and Los Angeles: University of California Press, 1978.

Kundera, Milan. *Immortality*. Translated by Peter Kussi. New York: Grove Weidenfeld, 1991.

Kuttner, Alfred Booth. "A Freudian Appreciation." In *D. H. Lawrence and "Sons and Lovers": Sources and Criticism*, edited by E. W. Tedlock, Jr., 76–100. New York: New York University Press, 1965.

Lacy, Dan. "The Economics of Publishing, or Adam Smith and Literature." In *The Sociology of Art and Literature*, edited by Milton C. Albrecht, James H. Barnett, and Mason Griff, 407–25. New York: Praeger, 1970.

Lane, Michael. *Books and Publishers*. Lexington, Mass.: D.C. Heath, 1980.

Lawrence, D. H. *Aaron's Rod*. Edited by Mara Kalnins. Cambridge: Cambridge University Press, 1988.

————. *Kangaroo*. Edited by Bruce Steele. Cambridge: Cambridge University Press, 1994.

————. *Lady Chatterley's Lover*. Edited by Michael Squires. Cambridge: Cambridge University Press, 1993.

————. *The Lost Girl*. Edited by John Worthen. Cambridge: Cambridge University Press, 1981.

————. *Mr Noon*. Edited by Lindeth Vasey. Cambridge: Cambridge University Press, 1984.

————. *The Plumed Serpent*. Edited by L. D. Clark. Cambridge: Cambridge University Press, 1987.

————. *The White Peacock*. London: Heinemann, 1962.

Leavis, F. R. "Mass Civilisation and Minority Culture." *For Continuity*. Freeport, N.Y.: Books for Libraries Press, 1968. 13–46. Rpt. 1933.

Leavis, Q. D. *Fiction and the Reading Public*. London: Chatto and Windus, 1965. Rpt. 1932.

Levenson, Michael H. *A Genealogy of Modernism: A Study of English Literary Doctrine 1908–1922*. Cambridge: Cambridge University Press, 1984.

Levin, Harry. *James Joyce: A Critical Introduction*. Norfolk: New Directions, 1941.

————. "What Was Modernism?" *Refractions*. New York: Oxford University Press, 1966, 271–95.

Lewes, George Henry. *The Principles of Success in Literature*. London and Felling-on-Tyne: Walter Scott Publishing, [1898].

Lidderdale, Jane and Mary Nicholson. *Dear Miss Weaver: Harriet Shaw Weaver 1876–1961.* New York: Viking, 1970.

Magalaner, Marvin and Richard M. Kain. *Joyce: The Man, the Work, the Reputation.* New York: New York University Press, 1956.

Mann, Peter H. "Books, Book Readers and Bookshops." In *Media Sociology,* edited by Jeremy Tunstall, 351–62. Urbana: University of Illinois Press, 1970.

McAlmon, Robert. *Being Geniuses Together.* Garden City, N.Y.: Doubleday, 1968.

Menand, Louis. *Discovering Modernism: T. S. Eliot and His Context.* New York: Oxford University Press, 1987.

Meyers, Jeffrey. *D. H. Lawrence.* New York: Knopf, 1990.

Moore, Harry T. *The Intelligent Heart.* New York: Farrar, Straus and Young, 1954.

————. *The Priest of Love: A Life of D. H. Lawrence.* New York: Farrar, Straus and Giroux, 1974.

Moscato, Michael and Leslie LeBlanc, eds. *The United States of America v. One Book Entitled "Ulysses" by James Joyce.* Frederick, Md.: University Publications of America, 1984.

Mudge, Bradford K. "The Man with Two Brains: Gothic Novels, Popular Culture, Literary History." *PMLA* 107 (1992): 92–104.

Najder, Zdzislaw. *Joseph Conrad: A Chronicle.* New Brunswick, N.J.: Rutgers University Press, 1983.

Ohmann, Richard. "The Shaping of a Canon: U.S. Fiction, 1960–1975." *Critical Inquiry* 10 (1983): 199–223.

Owen, Rodney Wilson. *James Joyce and the Beginnings of "Ulysses."* Ann Arbor, Mich.: UMI Research Press, 1983.

Peters, Joan D. "The Living and the Dead: Lawrence's Theory of the Novel and the Structure of *Lady Chatterley's Lover.*" *The D. H. Lawrence Review* 20 (1988): 5–20.

Peterson, Richard F. and Alan M. Cohn. "James Job: The Critical Reception of Joyce's Letters." *James Joyce Quarterly* 19 (1982): 429–40.

Pinker Papers (Papers of James B. Pinker and Sons, Literary Agents), McCormick Library of Special Collections, Northwestern University Library, Evanston, Illinois.

Pinkney, Tony. *D. H. Lawrence and Modernism.* Iowa City: University of Iowa Press, 1990.

Poggioli, Renato. "The Artist in the Modern World." In *The Sociology of Art and Literature,* edited by Milton C. Albrecht, James H. Barnett, and Mason Griff, 669–86. New York: Praeger Publishers, 1970.

Rabinowitz, Peter J. *Before Reading.* Ithaca, N.Y.: Cornell University Press, 1987.

Rainey, Lawrence S. "The Price of Modernism: Reconsidering the Publication of *The Waste Land*." *The Yale Review* 78 (1989): 279–300.

Randall, Dale B. J. *Joseph Conrad and Warrington Dawson: The Record of a Friendship*. Durham, N.C.: Duke University Press, 1968.

Read, Forrest, ed. *Pound/Joyce: The Letters of Ezra Pound to James Joyce, with Pound's Essays on Joyce*. New York: New Directions, 1967.

Riquelme, John Paul. *Teller and Tale in Joyce's Fiction*. Baltimore and London: Johns Hopkins University Press, 1983.

Rogers, Mary F. *Novels, Novelists, and Readers: Toward a Phenomenological Sociology of Literature*. Albany: State University of New York Press, 1991.

Rose, W. K., ed. *Letters of Wyndham Lewis*. London: Methuen, 1963.

Rothblatt, Sheldon. *The Revolution of the Dons: Cambridge and Society in Victorian England*. New York: Basic Books, 1968.

Rylance, Rick. "Lawrence's Politics." In *Rethinking Lawrence*, edited by Keith Brown, 163–80. Philadelphia: Open University Press, 1990.

Shrubb, E. P. "Reading *Sons and Lovers*." In *D. H. Lawrence's "Sons and Lovers*," edited by Harold Bloom, 109–30. New York: Chelsea House, 1988.

Sicker, Philip. "Surgery for the Novel: Lawrence's *Mr Noon* and the "Gentle Reader." *D. H. Lawrence Review* 20 (1988): 191–207.

Siegel, Carol. *Lawrence among the Women*. Charlottesville and London: University Press of Virginia, 1991.

Spilka, Mark. "Counterfeit Loves." In *D. H. Lawrence and "Sons and Lovers": Sources and Criticism*, edited by E. W. Tedlock, Jr., 200–16. New York: New York University Press, 1965.

Squires, Michael. *The Creation of "Lady Chatterley's Lover."* Baltimore and London: Johns Hopkins University Press, 1983.

Strychacz, Thomas. *Modernism, Mass Culture, and Professionalism*. New York: Cambridge University Press, 1993.

Sutherland, John A. "Fiction and the Erotic Cover." *Critical Quarterly* 33, no. 2 (1991): 3–36.

———. *Victorian Novelists and Publishers*. Chicago and London: University of Chicago Press, 1976.

Symons, Julian. *Makers of the New: The Revolution in Literature, 1912–1939*. London: André Deutsch Limited, 1987.

Torgovnick, Marianna. *Gone Primitive: Savage Intellects, Modern Lives*. Chicago and London: University of Chicago Press, 1990.

Unseld, Siegfried. *The Author and His Publisher*. Translated by Hunter Hannum and Hildegarde Hannum. Chicago and London: University of Chicago Press, 1980.

Unwin, Sir Stanley. *The Truth about a Publisher.* London: George Allen and Unwin, 1960.

Van Ghent, Dorothy. "On *Sons and Lovers.*" In *D. H. Lawrence's "Sons and Lovers,"* edited by Harold Bloom, 5–22. New York: Chelsea House, 1988.

Vasey, Lindeth. "Introduction." In *Mr Noon,* xix–xli. Cambridge: Cambridge University Press, 1984.

Viala, Alain. "Prismatic Effects." Translated by Paula Wissing. *Critical Inquiry* 14 (1988): 563–73.

Walters, Ray. "The Coming of the Computer." *New York Times Book Review,* 24 July 1983: 12–13.

Warhol, Robyn R. "Toward a Theory of the Engaging Narrator: Earnest Interventions in Gaskell, Stowe, and Eliot." *PMLA* 101 (1986): 811–18.

Watt, Ian. *Conrad in the Nineteenth Century.* Berkeley and Los Angeles: University of California Press, 1979.

Weiss, Daniel A. "The Mother in the Mind." In *D. H. Lawrence and "Sons and Lovers": Sources and Criticism,* edited by E. W. Tedlock, Jr., 112–36. New York: New York University Press, 1965.

Wilde, Oscar. "The Critic as Artist." In *The Collected Works of Oscar Wilde,* edited by Robert Ross. Vol. 8, 99–224. London: Routledge, 1993.

Woolsey, John M. "Decision." Reprinted in *Ulysses,* vii–xv. New York: Random House, 1961.

Worthen, John. *D. H. Lawrence and the Idea of the Novel.* Totowa, N.J.: Rowman and Littlefield, 1979.

———. *D. H. Lawrence: The Early Years, 1885-1912.* Cambridge: Cambridge University Press, 1991.

Index